# A TREASURY OF
# GERMAN
# BALLADS

*Bilingual Edition*

With English translations by
Helen Kurz Roberts and others

FREDERICK UNGAR PUBLISHING CO.
*NEW YORK*

# TABLE OF CONTENTS

## Adalbert von Chamisso (1781-1838)

## Ludwig Uhland (1787-1862)

## Friedrich Rückert (1788-1866)

## August von Platen (1796-1835)

## Heinrich Heine (1797-1856)

## August Kopisch (1799-1853)

# A TREASURY OF GERMAN BALLADS

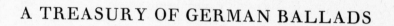

*Gottfried August Bürger*

## LENORE

Lenore fuhr ums Morgenrot
Empor aus schweren Träumen:
„Bist untreu, Wilhelm, oder tot?
Wie lange willst du säumen?" –
Er war mit König Friedrichs Macht
Gezogen in die Prager Schlacht
Und hatte nicht geschrieben,
Ob er gesund geblieben.

Der König und die Kaiserin,
Des langen Haders müde,
Erweichten ihren harten Sinn
Und machten endlich Friede;
Und jedes Heer, mit Sing und Sang,
Mit Paukenschlag und Kling und Klang,
Geschmückt mit grünen Reisern,
Zog heim zu seinen Häusern.

Und überall, allüberall,
Auf Wegen und auf Stegen,
Zog alt und jung dem Jubelschall
Der Kommenden entgegen.
„Gottlob!" rief Kind und Gattin laut,
„Willkommen!" manche frohe Braut;
Ach! aber für Lenoren
War Gruß und Kuß verloren.

Sie frug den Zug wohl auf und ab
Und frug nach allen Namen;
Doch keiner war, der Kundschaft gab,

LENORE

Lenore awoke when skies were red,
Of grievous dreams complaining:
"Art faithless, William, now – or dead?
Too long away remaining!"
With Frederick King of Prussia's might
He'd marched to Prague to bravely fight.
The silence was unbroken.

The King and Austria's Empress too
Of quarreling were tired;
They pity on their people knew,
And both now peace desired;
The soldiers all sang merry songs,
With cornets, drums and clash of gongs,
With branches green so gaily
Came ever nearer daily.

And everywhere from everywhere
On roads and bypaths winding,
Both young and old came marching there,
Their dearly loved ones finding.
"Praise God!" both wives and children cried,
And "Welcome!" many a happy bride.
Lenore's belov'd was missing,
No greeting and no kissing.

She questioned here and questioned there,
For news of William seeking,
But none of those who present were

Von allen, so da kamen.
Als nun das Heer vorüber war,
Zerraufte sie das Rabenhaar
Und warf sich hin zur Erde
Mit wütiger Gebärde.


Die Mutter lief wohl hin zu ihr:
„Ach, daß sich Gott erbarme!
Du trautes Kind, was ist mit dir?" –
Und schloß sie in die Arme –
„O Mutter, Mutter, hin ist hin!
Nun fahre Welt und alles hin!
Bei Gott ist kein Erbarmen.
O weh, o weh mir Armen!" –


„Hilf Gott! hilf! Sieh uns gnädig an!
Kind, bet ein Vaterunser!
Was Gott tut, das ist wohlgetan,
Gott, Gott erbarmt sich unser!"
„O mutter! Mutter! eitler Wahn!
Gott hat an mir nicht wohlgetan!
Was half, was half mein Beten?
Nun ist's nicht mehr vonnöten."


„Hilf, Gott, hilf! Wer den Vater kennt,
Der weiß, er hilft den Kindern.
Das hochgelobte Sakrament
Wird deinen Jammer lindern." –
„O Mutter, Mutter, was mich brennt,
Das lindert mir kein Sakrament!
Kein Sakrament mag Leben
Den Toten wiedergeben." –

Of William could be speaking.
When now the host had marched away,
She tore her raven hair and lay
Upon the earth there moaning,
In rage and anger groaning.


But now her mother ran to see. . . .
"Oh God, do not forsake her!
My child, what has come over thee?"
Into her arms she takes her.
"Oh mother, mother, done is done!
I curse the world, the earth, the sun!
For God is me forsaking;
Alas, my poor heart's breaking!"


"Oh help us, God, and mercy show!
Child, pray for mercy on us!
Do not revile what God does so!
God will have pity on us."
"Oh mother, mother, all is vain!
God from me every hope has ta'en!
Of what avail my praying?
Is William with me staying?"


"The Father always help has sent,
His children's lot to brighten,
The high and holy sacrament
Thy grief and woe will lighten."
"Oh mother, flames that in me burn
No sacrament away will turn!
No sacrament can living
To those who died be giving."

„Hör, Kind! Wie, wenn der falsche Mann
Im fernen Ungarlande
Sich seines Glaubens abgetan
Zum neuen Ehebande?
Laß fahren, Kind, sein Herz dahin!
Er hat es nimmermehr Gewinn!
Wenn Seel' und Leib sich trennen,
Wird ihn sein Meineid brennen!" –

„O Mutter! Mutter! hin ist hin!
Verloren ist verloren!
Der Tod, der Tod ist mein Gewinn!
O wär ich nie geboren!
Lisch aus, mein Licht! auf ewig aus!
Stirb hin, stirb hin in Nacht und Graus!
Bei Gott ist kein Erbarmen;
O weh, o weh mir Armen!" –

„ Hilf, Gott, hilf! Geh nicht ins Gericht
Mit deinem armen Kinde!
Sie weiß nicht, was die Zunge spricht;
Behalt ihr nicht die Sünde!
Ach, Kind, vergiß dein irdisch Leid,
Und denk an Gott und Seligkeit!
So wird doch deiner Seelen
Der Bräutigam nicht fehlen" –

„O Mutter! was ist Seligkeit?
O Mutter! was ist Hölle?
Bei ihm, bei ihm ist Seligkeit,
Und ohne Wilhelm Hölle! –
Lisch aus, mein Licht, auf ewig aus!
Stirb hin, stirb hin in Nacht und Graus!
Ohn' ihn mag ich auf Erden,
Mag dort nicht selig werden" –

"Perhaps this man, whom thou dost mourn,
His faith has now forsaken,
From Hungary will ne'er return,
And there a wife has taken.
Oh let him go, thy grieving cease,
He'll never know a moment's peace;
When soul from body's parting
His conscience will be smarting."

"Oh mother, mother, done is done!
And lost is gone forever!
For death, for death is all I've won,
Such life is welcome never.
Forever may my light go out!
And may it die in night and rout!
For God has me forsaken,
And all from me has taken."

"Oh Lord, judge not! On Thee I call,
Judge not thy child severely!
She knows not what she says at all,
'Tis grief and sorrow, merely.
Oh child, forget thy earthly woe,
And think of where thy soul must go;
In heaven, then, believe me,
A bridegroom will receive thee."

"Oh mother, what is Paradise?
Oh mother, what's damnation?
With him, with him is Paradise,
And where he's not . . . damnation.
Forever let my light go out!
And may it die in night and rout!
For me there are no pleasures
In earth's or heaven's treasures."

So wütete Verzweifelung
Ihr in Gehirn und Adern.
Sie fuhr mit Gottes Vorsehung
Vermessen fort zu hadern,
Zerschlug den Busen und zerrang
Die Hand bis Sonnenuntergang,
Bis auf am Himmelsbogen
Die goldnen Sterne zogen.

Und außen, horch! gings trapp trapp trapp
Als wie von Rosses Hufen,
Und klirrend stieg ein Reiter ab
An des Geländers Stufen.
Und horch! und horch den Pfortenring,
Ganz lose, leise, klinglingling!
Dann kamen durch die Pforte
Vernehmlich diese Worte:

„Holla, holla! Tu auf, mein Kind!
Schläfst, Liebchen, oder wachst du?
Wie bist noch gegen mich gesinnt?
Und weinest oder lachst du?" –
„Ach, Wilhelm, du? – So spät bei Nacht?
Geweinet hab ich und gewacht;
Ach! großes Leid erlitten!
Wo kommst du hergeritten?" –

„Wir satteln nur um Mitternacht.
Weit ritt ich her von Böhmen:
Ich habe spät mich aufgemacht
Und will dich mit mir nehmen!" –
„Ach, Wilhelm, erst herein geschwind!
Den Hagedorn durchsaust der Wind,
Herein, in meinen Armen,
Herzliebster, zu erwarmen!"

And so dark rage and black despair
Her mind and body harried;
Her quarrel with God's all-loving care
Presumptuously she carried.
She wrung her hands and beat her breast
Until the sun had gone to rest,
Until the heavens darkling
With golden stars were sparkling.

But hear! Outside, a clop clop clop!
The sound is ever clearer;
The rider comes to jingling stop,
His steps now bring him nearer.
Oh hear, oh hear the door-bell ring
And softly, softly ding ding ding!
He did not knock but merely
These words were heard quite clearly:

"Hello! Hello! The door, my child!
Art waking, love, or sleeping?
Art thou in anger now or mild,
Art laughing, or art weeping?"
"Oh William, William, can it be?
I've wept so much I scarce can see;
Oh sorrow's with me biding!
Oh, whence hast thou come riding?"

"At midnight thou and I shall ride,
Bohemia's where I started.
I've ridden quickly to thy side,
And we'll no more be parted."
"Oh William, come in quickly, do!
The wind the hawthorn rages through.
In here it is not storming,
Thy limbs I'll soon be warming."

„Laß sausen durch den Hagedorn,
Laß sausen, Kind, laß sausen!
Der Rappe scharrt, es klirrt der Sporn;
Ich darf allhier nicht hausen.
Komm, schürze, spring und schwinge dich
Auf meinen Rappen hinter mich!
Muß heut noch hundert Meilen
Mit dir ins Brautbett eilen." –


„Ach, wolltest hundert Meilen noch
Mich heut ins Brautbett tragen?
Und horch, es brummt die Glocke noch,
Die elf schon angeschlagen." –
„Sieh hin, sieh her, der Mond scheint hell;
Wir und die Toten reiten schnell,
Ich bringe dich, zur Wette,
Noch heut ins Hochzeitbette." –


„Sag an, wo ist dein Kämmerlein?
Wo?, wie dein Hochzeitbettchen?" –
„Weit, weit von hier! Still, kühl und klein! –
Sechs Bretter und zwei Brettchen!" –
„Hats Raum für mich?" – „Für dich und mich!
Komm, schürze, spring und schwinge dich!
Die Hochzeitsgäste hoffen!
Die Kammer steht uns offen." –


Schön Liebchen schürzte, sprang und schwang
Sich auf das Roß behende;
Wohl um den trauten Reiter schlang
Sie ihre Lilienhände,
Und hurre hurre, hopp hopp hopp!
Gings fort in sausendem Galopp,
Daß Roß und Reiter schnoben
Und Kies und Funken stoben.

"Then let the wind howl through the hedge,
Let howl, lass, stronger, stronger!
The black horse paws, the spurs have edge,
I can't remain here longer.
Come dress and with a leap thou be
Upon the black horse here with me.
There's a hundred miles to cover
To joys of love and lover."

"A hundred miles must we away
Our bridal bed to sleep in?
Oh listen, night is on the way,
And here's a bed to creep in."
"See there! The moon shines clear and bright.
We and the dead ride fast tonight.
Midnight, I pledge will find us
The wedding rites behind us."

"Oh tell me, where's the little room,
The bed that I've a share of?"
"Far, far from here, cool silent tomb,
Six planks, small boards a pair of."
"There's room for me?" "For me and thee!
Come hurry, dress and ride with me.
The wedding guests are waiting,
Our nuptials celebrating."

She dressed herself, to horse she swung,
Onto the horse beside her;
Her soft white arms she straightway flung
Around the urgent rider.
And hurry, hurry, hop hop hop!
In reckless gallop, clop clop clop!
The snorting steed was speeding
Through stones and sparks unheeding.

Zur rechten und zur linken Hand,
Vorbei vor ihren Blicken,
Wie flogen Anger, Heid' und Land!
Wie donnerten die Brücken! –
,,Graut Liebchen auch? – der Mond scheint hell!
Hurra! die Toten reiten schnell!
Graut Liebchen auch vor Toten?'' –
,,Ach nein! – Doch laß die Toten!'' –

Was klang dort für Gesang und Klang?
Was flatterten die Raben? –
Horch Glockenklang! Horch Totensang:
,,Laßt uns den Leib begraben!''
Und näher zog ein Leichenzug,
Der Sarg und Totenbahre trug.
Das Lied war zu vergleichen
Dem Unkenruf in Teichen.

,,Nach Mitternacht begrabt den Leib
Mit Klang und Sang und Klage!
Jetzt führ ich heim mein junges Weib.
Mit, mit zum Brautgelage!
Komm, Küster, hier! komm mit dem Chor
Und gurgle mir das Brautlied vor!
Komm, Pfaff, und sprich den Segen.
Eh wir zu Bett uns legen!'' –

Still Klang und Sang – die Bahre schwand.
Gehorsam seinem Rufen
Kams, hurre! hurre! nachgerannt
Hart hinters Rappen Hufen.
Und immer weiter, hopp hopp hopp!
Gings fort in sausendem Galopp,
Daß Roß und Reiter schnoben
Und Kies und Funken stoben.

As they rode on, on either hand
Before their eyes were flashing
The flying turf and heath and land,
And hoofs on bridges crashing.
"Art thou afraid? The moon shines bright!
Hurrah! the dead ride fast tonight!
Art thou afraid of dead men?"
"Let be, let be the dead men!"

What song rang out the road along?
And flutter here the ravens?
Hear! Clang of bells! Hear! Burial song!
"The dead to their last havens!"
A burial party nearer drew,
A bier and coffin bore the crew.
Their singing was appalling,
Like frogs in sedge-pools calling.

"Now dig the grave when midnight's past,
With clang and song and wailing;
With my young bride I'm riding fast,
Let not the feast be failing.
Come, sexton, here! Bring all along!
And gurgle out the bridal song.
Come, priest and speak the blessing.
'Tis late and time is pressing."

The bier falls back . . . still clang and song. . . .
His urgent call obeying,
And hurry, hurry, ran along
Behind the black horse staying.
And farther, farther, hop hop hop!
The black horse galloped, clop clop clop!
The snorting steed was speeding,
Through sparks and stones unheeding.

Wie flogen rechts, wie flogen links
Gebirge, Bäum' und Hecken!
Wie flogen links und rechts und links
Die Dörfer, Städt' und Flecken! –
„Graut Liebchen auch? – Der Mond scheint hell!
Hurra! die Toten reiten schnell!
Graut Liebchen auch vor Toten?" –
„Ach! laß sie ruhn, die Toten!" –

Sieh da! sieh da! Am Hochgericht
Tanzt um des Rades Spindel
Halb sichtbarlich bei Mondenlicht
Ein luftiges Gesindel.
„Sa! sa! Gesindel! hier! komm hier!
Gesindel, komm und folge mir!
Tanz uns den Hochzeitsreigen,
Wenn wir zu Bette steigen!" –

Und das Gesindel husch husch husch!
Kam hinten nachgeprasselt,
Wie Wirbelwind am Haselbusch
Durch dürre Blätter rasselt.
Und weiter, weiter, hopp hopp hopp!
Gings fort in sausendem Galopp,
Daß Roß und Reiter schnoben
Und Kies und Funken stoben.

Wie flog, was rund der Mond beschien,
Wie flog es in die Ferne!
Wie flogen oben überhin
Der Himmel und die Sterne! –
„Graut Liebchen auch? – der Mond scheint hell!
Hurra! die Toten reiten schnell!
Graut Liebchen auch vor Toten?" –
„O weh! laß ruhn die Toten!". . .

Now flew to right, now flew to left
The hedges, trees and mountains;
Now flew to left and right and left
Towns, cities, village fountains.
"Art thou afraid? The moon shines bright!
Hurrah! the dead ride fast tonight!
Art thou afraid of dead men?"
"Let rest, let rest the dead men!"

By scaffold high . . . a ghastly sight. . . .
Around a wheel there dancing,
Half visible in pale moonlight,
A ghostly crew is prancing.
"Hello, there! Devil's crew, come here!
Come, follow coffin and the bier!
For wedding dance we're yearning,
Our hearts for love are burning."

And that black crew then rush rush rush!
Came rattling on and hustling,
As whirlpool through a hazelbush
Goes through the dry leaves rustling.
And farther, farther, hop hop hop!
The black horse galloped, clop clop clop
The snorting steed was speeding
Through sparks and stones unheeding.

And all on which the pale moon shone
Soon far away was flying;
The sky and stars were likewise gone,
The rider madly crying:
"Art thou afraid? The moon shines bright!
Hurrah! the dead ride fast tonight!
Art thou afraid of dead men?"
"Woe's me, let rest the dead men!"

„Rapp'! Rapp'! Mich dünkt, der Hahn schon ruft...
Bald wird der Sand verrinnen...
Rapp'! Rapp'! ich wittre Morgenluft...
Rapp'! tummle dich von hinnen!
Vollbracht, vollbracht ist unser Lauf!
Das Hochzeitbette tut sich auf!
Die Toten reiten schnelle!
Wir sind, wir sind zur Stelle."–

Rasch auf ein eisern Gittertor
Gings mit verhängtem Zügel;
Mit schwanker Gert ein Schlag davor
Zersprengte Schloß und Riegel.
Die Flügel flogen klirrend auf,
Und über Gräber ging der Lauf;
Es blinkten Leichensteine
Rundum im Mondenscheine.

Ha sieh! Ha sieh! Im Augenblick,
Hu! hu! ein gräßlich Wunder!
Des Reiters Koller, Stück für Stück,
Fiel ab wie mürber Zunder,
Zum Schädel ohne Zopf und Schopf,
Zum nackten Schädel ward sein Kopf,
Sein Körper zum Gerippe
Mit Stundenglas und Hippe.

Hoch bäumte sich, wild schnob der Rapp'
Und sprühte Feuerfunken;
Und hui! wars unter ihr hinab
Verschwunden und versunken.
Geheul! Geheul aus hoher Luft,
Gewinsel kam aus tiefer Gruft.
Lenorens Herz mit Beben
Rang zwischen Tod und Leben.

"Come, Black, methinks the cock now crows,
The sand is quickly draining.
Black! Black! The morning light now grows!
Black, hurry! Time is waning!
Our ride is finished, now is past,
We've reached the bridal bed at last.
Ah, how the dead ride madly!
The bed we welcome gladly."

The horse now went with pace full slow
To an iron gate, and wonder
Of wonders! soon a gentle blow
Tore lock and bolt asunder.
The gate with creaking opened wide,
And over graves they went inside,
The gravestones there all seeming
To glare in the moonlight gleaming.

But see! Will wonders never cease?
Oh horror misbegotten!
The rider's doublet piece by piece
Fell off like tinder rotten.
Without his hair his brain-pan there
Became a naked skull and bare,
His skeleton full mickle
With hour-glass and sickle.

The snorting horse reared up for flight,
Far sparks of fire sending,
And in a trice was gone from sight,
Into the depths descending.
And howling came from out the air,
And moaning from the black depths there.
Lenore's heart was abreaking,
For death its toll was taking.

Nun tanzten wohl bei Mondenglanz
Rundum herum im Kreise
Die Geister einen Kettentanz
Und heulten diese Weise:
„Geduld! Geduld! Wenns Herz auch bricht!
Mit Gott im Himmel hadre nicht!
Des Leibes bist du ledig;
Gott sei der Seele gnädig!"

And dancing, while the moon shone bright,
Their rounds of death and mourning,
The spirits sang from depth and height
In howling tones this warning:
"Resign! Resign! Though hearts may rend!
'Gainst God in Heaven do not fend!
Your life on earth has ended.
In God's grace be commended!"

*Francis Owen*

*Johann Wolfgang von Goethe*

DER SÄNGER

„Was hör ich draußen vor dem Tor,
Was auf der Brücke schallen?
Laß den Gesang vor unserm Ohr
Im Saale widerhallen!"
Der König sprachs, der Page lief;
Der Knabe kam, der König rief:
„Laßt mir herein den Alten!"

„Gegrüßet seid mir, edle Herrn,
Gegrüßt ihr, schöne Damen!
Welch reicher Himmel! Stern bei Stern!
Wer kennet ihre Namen?
Im Saal voll Pracht und Herrlichkeit
Schließt, Augen, euch: hier ist nicht Zeit,
Sich staunend zu ergötzen."

Der Sänger drückt' die Augen ein
Und schlug in vollen Tönen;
Die Ritter schauten mutig drein
Und in den Schoß die Schönen.
Der König, dem das Lied gefiel,
Ließ, ihn zu ehren für sein Spiel,
Eine goldne Kette reichen.

„Die goldne Kette gib mir nicht,
Die Kette gib den Rittern,
Vor deren kühnem Angesicht

## THE BARD

"Beyond the gate, what do I hear
Upon the bridge resounding?
Within my hall, before my ear
The song shall be rebounding!"
The king he spoke, the page he sped,
The boy returned, the ruler said:
"Let in the ancient singer!"

"Be greeted ladies, fair ye are,
I greet ye men of station!
What splendid heaven, star on star!
Who names such constellation?
Fall shut, mine eyes; ye have no time
This hall's magnificence sublime,
Astonished to admire."

The singer closed his eyes and played
Resounding tunes and rare ones;
The knights were looking unafraid,
Demurely glanced the fair ones.
The king, well pleased, exclaimed: "I deem
To him, as sign of my esteem,
A golden chain be given."

"Give not to me this chain of gold,
But to some knight as token,
Before whose countenance so bold,

Der Feinde Lanzen splittern;
Gib sie dem Kanzler, den du hast,
Und laß ihn noch die goldne Last
Zu andern Lasten tragen.

Ich singe, wie der Vogel singt,
Der in den Zweigen wohnet;
Das Lied, das aus der Kehle dringt,
Ist Lohn, der reichlich lohnet.
Doch darf ich bitten, bitt ich eins:
Laß mir den besten Becher Weins
In purem Golde reichen."

Er setzt' ihn an, er trank ihn aus:
„O Trank voll süßer Labe!
O wohl dem hochbeglückten Haus,
Wo das ist kleine Gabe!
Ergehts euch wohl, so denkt an mich,
Und danket Gott so warm, als ich
Für diesen Trunk euch danke."

The enemy's lance is broken.
Or to thy chancellor of state
And let him add its golden weight
To other loads he carries.

"I sing as sings the bird that lives
In trees and never hoardeth.
The song the throat pours forth, it gives
Reward that well rewardeth.
Yet if I may, I this request:
To me a cup of wine, thy best,
In purest gold, be offered."

He raised it, drained it to the lees;
"Refresher, sweet and mighty!
Well blest the house where gifts like these
Are trifles, rated lightly.
If ye fare well, so think of me
And thank the Lord as heartily
As for this drink I thank ye."

*Helen Kurz Roberts*

## DIE BRAUT VON KORINTH

Nach Korinthus von Athen gezogen
Kam ein Jüngling, dort noch unbekannt.
Einen Bürger hofft' er sich gewogen:
Beide Väter waren gastverwandt,
    Hatten frühe schon
    Töchterchen und Sohn
Braut und Bräutigam voraus genannt.

Aber wird er auch willkommen scheinen,
Wenn er teuer nicht die Gunst erkauft?
Er ist noch ein Heide mit den Seinen,
Und sie sind schon Christen und getauft.
    Keimt ein Glaube neu,
    Wird oft Lieb und Treu
Wie ein böses Unkraut ausgerauft.

Und schon lag das ganze Haus im stillen,
Vater, Töchter, nur die Mutter wacht;
Sie empfängt den Gast mit bestem Willen,
Gleich ins Prunkgemach wird er gebracht.
    Wein und Essen prangt,
    Eh er es verlangt:
So versorgend wünscht sie gute Nacht.

Aber bei dem wohlbestellten Essen
Wird die Lust der Speise nicht erregt.
Müdigkeit läßt Speis und Trank vergessen,
Daß er angekleidet sich aufs Bette legt;
    Und er schlummert fast,
    Als ein seltner Gast
Sich zur offnen Tür hereinbewegt.

## THE BRIDE OF CORINTH

To Corinthus came, from Athens hailing,
Once a youth who, there unknown to most,
Hoped that townsman's aid would not be failing,
Who had been his father's guest and host.
At an early stage
When of tender age
Were the children pledgéd in a toast.

Will his welcome be with hesitations
If he cannot buy their favor prized?
He is pagan still, like his relations,
They are Christians, recently baptized.
When a creed is born,
Love and faith are torn
Often from the heart, like weeds despised.

Father, daughters, all the house is sleeping,
But the mother's lamp is still alight;
She receives the youth with friendly greeting,
To the guest room he is led forthright.
Food and wine are brought,
Even ere he thought;
All provided for, she bids good night.

But his taste for food is not excited,
Though a well-appointed meal is spread;
Food and drink by weariness are slighted,
Clothed he stretches out upon the bed;
But from sleep is wrest'
When so strange a guest
Enters through the door with silent tread.

Denn er sieht, bei seiner Lampe Schimmer
Tritt, mit weißem Schleier und Gewand,
Sittsam still ein Mädchen in das Zimmer,
Um die Stirn ein schwarz- und goldnes Band.
   Wie sie ihn erblickt,
   Hebt sie, die erschrickt,
Mit Erstaunen eine weiße Hand.


„Bin ich", rief sie aus, „so fremd im Hause,
Daß ich von dem Gaste nichts vernahm?
Ach, so hält man mich in meiner Klause!
Und nun überfällt mich hier die Scham.
   Ruhe nur so fort
   Auf dem Lager dort,
Und ich gehe schnell, so wie ich kam."


„Bleibe, schönes Mädchen!", ruft der Knabe,
Rafft von seinem Lager sich geschwind:
„Hier ist Ceres', hier ist Bacchus' Gabe,
Und du bringst den Amor, liebes Kind!
   Bist vor Schrecken blaß!
   Liebe, komm und laß,
Laß uns sehn, wie froh die Götter sind!"


„Ferne bleib, o Jüngling, bleibe stehen!
Ich gehöre nicht den Freuden an.
Schon der letzte Schritt ist, ach, geschehen
Durch der guten Mutter kranken Wahn,
   Die genesend schwur:
   Jugend und Natur
Sei dem Himmel künftig untertan.

In the glimmer that his lamp is throwing
Stands revealed a maid, demurely bland,
White her veil and white her garments flowing,
Round her head a black and golden band.
At his sudden sight,
She lifts up with fright
And astonishment a snow-white hand.

"Am I here a stranger, guests are bidden
To this house and I ignore their name?
Ah, they keep me in my cell, well hidden!
Here I stand now, overcome with shame.
To resume thy rest
On this couch is best,
And I leave as quickly as I came."

"Fairest maiden! Canst thou stay?" he queries.
From the couch he rises speedily;
"Here is Bacchus' gift and here is Ceres',
Amor, dearest child, is brought by thee!
Pale thou art, upset,
Dearest, come and let,
Let us see how glad the gods can be!"

"Stay away, O youth, by luck forsaken,
For the joys of life I am unfit.
Ah, the final step, it has been taken
By my ailing mother's clouded wit,
Who recov'ring vowed:
Nature should be cowed,
Youth, in future, must to heav'n submit.

Und der alten Götter bunt Gewimmel
Hat sogleich das stille Haus geleert.
Unsichtbar wird einer nur im Himmel,
Und ein Heiland wird am Kreuz verehrt;
    Opfer fallen hier,
    Weder Lamm noch Stier,
Aber Menschenopfer unerhört."


Und er fragt und wäget alle Worte,
Deren keines seinem Geist entgeht:
„Ist es möglich, daß am stillen Orte
Die geliebte Braut hier vor mir steht?
    Sei die meine nur!
    Unsrer Väter Schwur
Hat vom Himmel Segen uns erfleht."


„Mich erhältst du nicht, du gute Seele!
Meiner zweiten Schwester gönnt man dich.
Wenn ich mich in stiller Klause quäle,
Ach, in ihren Armen denk an mich,
    Die an dich nur denkt,
    Die sich liebend kränkt;
In die Erde bald verbirgt sie sich."


„Nein, bei dieser Flamme seis geschworen,
Gütig zeigt sie Hymen uns voraus:
Bist der Freude nicht und mir verloren,
Kommst mit mir in meines Vaters Haus.
    Liebchen, bleibe hier!
    Feire gleich mit mir
Unerwartet unsern Hochzeitsschmaus!"

"Of the ancient gods, in gay profusion,
Voided was the house for evermore.
One unseen, in heavenly seclusion,
On the cross, a saviour, they adore;
Sacrificed are here,
Neither lamb nor steer,
But the human victims by the score."

Then he asks and weighs what she is saying.
Not a word escapes his mind intent:
"Could it be that here I am surveying
Her, who for my dearest bride was meant?
Shouldst be mine anow!
For our fathers' vow
Grants us heaven's blessing and assent."

"Thou, my love, wilt not obtain me, never!
For my sister they have destined thee.
In my silent cell I pine forever,
Ah, when in her arms, remember me,
Whom thy sight does thrill,
Who for love is ill,
In the earth she soon will hidden be."

"No! and by this flame that Hymen lighted
Kindly in advance for us, I swear:
Art not lost to joy or me; united
To my father's house we shall repair.
Stay with me, my dear!
Unexpected here
We may celebrate our wedding fare!"

Und schon wechseln sie der Treue Zeichen:
Golden reicht sie ihm die Kette dar,
Und er will ihr eine Schale reichen,
Silbern, künstlich, wie nicht eine war.
    „Die ist nicht für mich;
    Doch, ich bitte dich,
Eine Locke gib von deinem Haar."

Eben schlug die dumpfe Geisterstunde,
Und nun schien es ihr erst wohl zu sein.
Gierig schlürfte sie mit blassem Munde
Nun den dunkel blutgefärbten Wein;
    Doch vom Weizenbrot,
    Das er freundlich bot,
Nahm sie nicht den kleinsten Bissen ein.

Und dem Jüngling reichte sie die Schale,
Der, wie sie, nun hastig lüstern trank.
Liebe fordert er beim stillen Mahle:
Ach, sein armes Herz war liebekrank!
    Doch sie widersteht,
    Wie er immer fleht,
Bis er weinend auf das Bette sank.

Und sie kommt und wirft sich zu ihm nieder:
„Ach, wie ungern seh ich dich gequält!
Aber, ach, berührst du meine Glieder,
Fühlst du schaudernd, was ich dir verhehlt.
    Wie der Schnee so weiß,
    Aber kalt wie Eis
Ist das Liebchen, das du dir erwählt."

Pledges of their troth ere long they offer;
She gives him a golden chain to wear,
He presents her with a precious coffer,
Wrought in silver and without compare.
"This is not for me;
But I beg of thee,
Let me have a ringlet of thy hair."

Midnight struck, the hour when ghosts are slinking,
Only now she seemed released from strain.
Pale-mouthed, avidly she started drinking
Wine, as dark and red as blood would stain;
Of the wheaten bread,
Though he gently pled,
E'en the smallest piece she did disdain.

To the youth she then a goblet proffered,
Who like her, with haste and relish drank.
Love he begged from her and love he offered;
"Ah, his love-sick heart was simple frank!
But she does not cede,
Though his passions plead,
Till he weeping on the pillows sank.

Then she throws herself beside him, kneeling:
"Ah! I hate the tortures I impose!
Should'st thou touch me though, thou wouldst be feeling
Shudd'ringly, what I must now disclose.
Marble-white of hue,
Cold as marble too
Is the maiden whom for love thou chose."

Heftig faßt er sie mit starken Armen,
Von der Liebe Jugendkraft durchmannt:
„Hoffe doch bei mir noch zu erwarmen,
Wärst du selbst mir aus dem Grab gesandt!"
   Wechselhauch und Kuß!
   Liebesüberfluß!
„Brennst du nicht und fühlest mich entbrannt?"

Liebe schließet fester sie zusammen,
Tränen mischen sich in ihre Lust;
Gierig saugt sie seines Mundes Flammen,
Eins ist nur im andern sich bewußt.
   Seine Liebeswut
   Wärmt ihr starres Blut,
Doch es schlägt kein Herz in ihrer Brust.

Unterdessen schleichet auf dem Gange
Häuslich spät die Mutter noch vorbei,
Horchet an der Tür und horchet lange,
Welch ein sonderbarer Ton es sei:
   Klag- und Wonnelaut,
   Bräutigams und Braut,
Und des Liebesstammelns Raserei!

Unbeweglich bleibt sie an der Türe,
Weil sie erst sich überzeugen muß,
Und sie hört die höchsten Liebesschwüre,
Lieb- und Schmeichelworte, mit Verdruß:
   „Still! der Hahn erwacht!" –
   „Aber morgen nacht
Bist du wieder da?" – und Kuß auf Kuß.

Strong of arm, he grasps her passionately,
Love's young power fills his manly frame:
"Hope thou still! My nearness warms thee greatly,
Wert thou even one the grave could claim!"
Breath-exchange and kiss,
Love's excess and bliss!
"Art thou burning, canst thou feel my flame?"

Love is binding them and strong desire,
Tears are mingling with their ecstasies;
Ardently she drinks his breath of fire,
Each one sentient through the other's bliss.
Though his frenzy could
Warm her frozen blood,
In her breast, no heartbeat answers his.

On her nightly round, from somewhere yonder,
Steals the mother through the gallery,
Listens at the door with growing wonder,
What this odd, mysterious sound might be:
Bride and groom the twain,
Voicing joy and pain,
Stammering with love-crazed urgency.

Stealthily about the door she hovers,
Making sure that something is amiss,
Vexed, she hears the greatest oaths of lovers,
Words of coaxing, words of love and bliss.
"Hark the cock crows – light!
But tomorrow night
Wilt thou come again?" – and kiss on kiss.

Länger hält die Mutter nicht das Zürnen,
Öffnet das bekannte Schloß geschwind:
„Gibt es hier im Hause solche Dirnen,
Die dem Fremden gleich zu Willen sind?"
     So zur Tür hinein.
     Bei der Lampe Schein
Sieht sie – Gott!, sie sieht ihr eigen Kind.

Und der Jüngling will im ersten Schrecken
Mit des Mädchens eignem Schleierflor,
Mit dem Teppich die Geliebte decken,
Doch sie windet gleich sich selbst hervor.
     Wie mit Geists Gewalt
     Hebet die Gestalt
Lang und langsam sich im Bett empor.

„Mutter! Mutter!", spricht sie hohle Worte,
„So mißgönnt Ihr mir die schöne Nacht!
Ihr vertreibt mich von dem warmen Orte,
Bin ich zur Verzweiflung nur erwacht?
     Ists Euch nicht genug,
     Daß ins Leichentuch,
Daß Ihr früh mich in das Grab gebracht?

Aber aus der schwerbedeckten Enge
Treibet mich ein eigenes Gericht.
Eurer Priester summende Gesänge
Und ihr Segen haben kein Gewicht;
     Salz und Wasser kühlt
     Nicht, wo Jugend fühlt;
Ach, die Erde kühlt die Liebe nicht!

But the mother, past endurance, wrenches
Ope the lock familiar to her.
"Does this building shelter whoring wenches,
Ready every stranger's bed to share?"
Enters thus the room,
In the lamplight's gloom
Sees, oh God! she sees her daughter there.

In his sudden fright, the youthful lover
Tries the flimsy veil the maid has shed,
Tries the carpet for his love as cover,
She unwinds, at once, what he has spread.
As with ghostly might,
To her fullest height,
Slowly she lifts up her form in bed.

"Mother," says she – hollow sounds her chiding –
"Thou dost grudge a night beside my groom!
Thou dost drive me from this cosy biding,
Have I wakened only to my doom?
Not enough thou vowed
Me into the shroud,
And so soon hast brought me to the tomb?

"But by higher judgment I am driven
From my heavy-lidded, narrow berth.
And the sing-song of thy priests has given
No relief; their blessing has no worth;
Salt and water soothe
Not the zest of youth;
Ah, love's ardor is not cooled by earth!

Dieser Jüngling war mir erst versprochen,
Als noch Venus' heitrer Tempel stand.
Mutter, habt Ihr doch das Wort gebrochen,
Weil ein fremd, ein falsch Gelübd' Euch band!
   Doch kein Gott erhört,
   Wenn die Mutter schwört,
Zu versagen ihrer Tochter Hand.


Aus dem Grabe werd ich ausgetrieben,
Noch zu suchen das vermißte Gut,
Noch den schon verlornen Mann zu lieben
Und zu saugen seines Herzens Blut.
   Ists um den geschehn,
   Muß nach andern gehn,
Und das junge Volk erliegt der Wut.


Schöner Jüngling, kannst nicht länger leben!
Du versiechest nun an diesem Ort.
Meine Kette hab ich dir gegeben;
Deine Locke nehm ich mit mir fort.
   Sieh sie an genau!
   Morgen bist du grau,
Und nur braun erscheinst du wieder dort.


Höre, Mutter, nun die letzte Bitte:
Einen Scheiterhaufen schichte du!
Öffne meine bange kleine Hütte,
Bring in Flammen Liebende zur Ruh!
   Wenn der Funke sprüht,
   Wenn die Asche glüht,
Eilen wir den alten Göttern zu."

"He, this youth, was pledged to me by token,
When still Venus' temples graced the land.
But thy word, O mother, thou hast broken,
At a false, and foreign vow's command!
Yet no god forbears
When a mother swears,
To refuse her daughter's promised hand.

"From the silent graveyard I am driven,
Still to seek the joys I missed, – though dust – ,
Still to love him, who from me was riven,
Suck his life-blood from his heart with gust.
Once he is destroyed,
Others are decoyed,
And the young fall victims to my lust.

"Handsome youth, to death thou hast awoken!
Thou wilt pine away here, in despond.
I have given thee my chain as token,
And I take thy lock of hair as bond.
Look at it today,
Morrow finds thee gray,
Brown-haired thou appear'st in the beyond.

"Mother, this my last wish, is compelling:
Build a pyre! Let this be thy aim!
Open up my small and narrow dwelling,
Lay the lovers to their rest in flame!
While the sparks still fly,
Ere the embers die,
We, above, the ancient gods acclaim."

*Helen Kurz Roberts*

## DER TOTENTANZ

Der Türmer, der schaut zu Mitten der Nacht
Hinab auf die Gräber in Lage;
Der Mond, der hat alles ins Helle gebracht,
Der Kirchhof, er liegt wie am Tage.
Da regt sich ein Grab und ein anderes dann:
Sie kommen hervor, ein Weib da, ein Mann,
In weißen und schleppenden Hemden.

Das reckt nun, es will sich ergetzen sogleich,
Die Knöchel zur Runde, zum Kranze,
So arm und so jung, und so alt und so reich;
Doch hindern die Schleppen am Tanze.
Und weil hier die Scham nun nicht weiter gebeut,
So schütteln sich alle, da liegen zerstreut
Die Hemdelein über den Hügeln.

Nun hebt sich der Schenkel, nun wackelt das Bein,
Gebärden da gibt es vertrackte;
Dann klipperts und klapperts mitunter hinein,
Als schlüg man die Hölzlein zum Takte.
Das kommt nun dem Türmer so lächerlich vor!
Da raunt ihm der Schalk, der Versucher, ins Ohr:
Geh, hole dir einen der Laken!

Getan wie gedacht! und er flüchtet sich schnell
Nun hinter geheiligte Türen.
Der Mond, und noch immer er scheinet so hell
Zum Tanz, den sie schauderlich führen.
Doch endlich verlieret sich dieser und der,
Schleicht eins nach dem andern gekleidet einher,
Und husch! ist es unter dem Rasen.

## DANCE MACABRE

At midnight the warden is looking around,
And down where the grave mounds are sited.
The moon has been brightening all on the ground,
Like noon is the churchyard thus lighted.
A grave now is stirring, another one then:
They start to come forth, the women, the men,
In yellow-white, long-trailing cerements.

They stretch, they are feeling for pleasure an itch,
Their ankles for round dance and lancers,
Thus poor and thus young and thus old and thus rich,
But trains are a hindrance to dancers.
As shame here no longer commands to the crowds
They shake themselves all, and thereafter the shrouds
Lie scattered all over the grave mounds.

Now thighs are uplifted, now legs are ashake,
In postures contorted at pleasure;
And clickings and clackings right into it break,
Like batons when beating a measure.
How ludicrous all to the warden appears!
The tempter, the rogue is assailing his ears:
Go out and get one of the grave clothes!

No sooner 'tis said than 'tis done, and with speed
He flees behind sanctified portals.
The moon is still shining so bright, as they lead
Their dances, abhorrent to mortals.
Yet finally this one, then that one falls out,
Creeps one after t'other enshrouded about
And hush! it is under its grass plot.

Nur einer, der trippelt und stolpert zuletzt
Und tappet und grapst an den Grüften;
Doch hat kein Geselle so schwer ihn verletzt:
Er wittert das Tuch in den Lüften.
Er rüttelt die Turmtür, sie schlägt ihn zurück.
Geziert und gesegnet, dem Türmer zum Glück;
Sie blinkt von metallenen Kreuzen.

Das Hemd muß er haben, da rastet er nicht,
Da gilt auch kein langes Besinnen;
Den gotischen Zierrat ergreift nun der Wicht
Und klettert von Zinne zu Zinnen.
Nun ists um den armen, den Türmer getan!
Es ruckt sich von Schnörkel zu Schnörkel hinan,
Langbeinigen Spinnen vergleichbar.

Der Türmer erbleichet, der Türmer erbebt,
Gern gäb er ihn wieder, den Laken.
Da häkelt – jetzt hat er am längsten gelebt –
Den Zipfel ein eiserner Zacken.
Schon trübet der Mond sich, verschwindenden Scheins,
Die Glocke, sie donnert ein mächtiges Eins,
Und unten zerschellt das Gerippe.

One only, it stumbles and trips in alarm,
Is fumbling by tombstones and snatching;
But none of its comrades has done it such harm;
The shroud in the air it is smatching.
It rattles the door, which stands up to the test,
What luck for the warden! embellished and blest
It glitters metallic with crosses.

The shroud, it must have it, no rest for the sprite!
No time to reflect or enquire;
It clutches the Gothic adornments, the wight,
And clambers from spire to spire.
Poor warden, to find so untimely an end!
From stone scroll to stone scroll he sees it ascend
Alike to some long-legged spider.

The warden is paling, the warden is numb,
The shroud he is longing to render,
A corner however – his end must have come –
Is caught by some iron-wrought fender.
The moon, she is dimming, her lightening done,
The bell in the tower is thundering one,
Beneath him the skeleton splinters.

*Helen Kurz Roberts*

## ERLKÖNIG

Wer reitet so spät durch Nacht und Wind?
Es ist der Vater mit seinem Kind.
Er hat den Knaben wohl in dem Arm,
Er faßt ihn sicher, er hält ihn warm.

„Mein Sohn, was birgst du so bang dein Gesicht?"
„Siehst, Vater, du den Erlkönig nicht,
Den Erlenkönig mit Kron' und Schweif?"
„Mein Sohn, es ist ein Nebelstreif."

„Du liebes Kind, komm, geh mit mir!
Gar schöne Spiele spiel ich mit dir;
Manch bunte Blumen sind an dem Strand,
Meine Mutter hat manch gülden Gewand."

„Mein Vater, mein Vater, und hörest du nicht,
Was Erlenkönig mir leise verspricht!?"
„Sei ruhig, bleibe ruhig, mein Kind;
In dürren Blättern säuselt der Wind."

„Willst, feiner Knabe, du mit mir gehn?
Meine Töchter sollen dich warten schön;
Meine Töchter führen den nächtlichen Reihn
Und wiegen und tanzen und singen dich ein."

„Mein Vater, mein Vater, und siehst du nicht dort
Erlkönigs Töchter am düstern Ort?"
„Mein Sohn, mein Sohn, ich seh es genau,
Es scheinen die alten Weiden so grau."

## ELF-KING

Who's riding so late through night-wind wild?
It is the father with his child;
He holds his boy safe from the storm,
His cradling arm is keeping him warm.

"My son, why turn your face in fear?"
"Look, father! the Elf-king is so near —
The King of Elves with crown and cloak!"
"My son, it is a wisp of smoke."

"My darling child, do come with me:
I'll play such wondrous games with thee,
My shores have flowers manifold,
My mother'll dress thee in cloth of gold."

"My father, my father, oh don't you hear
What Elf-king's whispering in my ear?"
"Be still, you must stay still, my son:
The wind through withered leaves has spun."

"Do come with me, my lad so fair!
My lovely daughters shall give thee care,
Through night my daughters' revels sweep,
They'll dance and they'll sing and they'll rock thee to sleep."

"My father, my father, oh don't you behold
The Elf-king's daughters deep in the wold?"
"My son, my son, I see it full well:
Grey willows are rising in yonder dell."

„Ich liebe dich, mich reizt deine schöne Gestalt;
Und bist du nicht willig, so brauch ich Gewalt."
„Mein Vater, mein Vater, jetzt faßt er mich an!
Erlkönig hat mir ein Leids getan!"

Dem Vater grausets, er reitet geschwind,
Er hält in Armen das ächzende Kind,
Erreicht den Hof mit Mühe und Not –
In seinen Armen das Kind war tot.

"I love thee, I covet thy beautiful shape;
And comest thou not willing, I'll take thee by rape!"
"My father, my father, his touch is so chill!
The Elf-king, the Elf-king has done me an ill!"

The father makes haste, ashiver with fear;
He clasps in his arm his whimpering dear,
But when at last he reaches his stead
In his arm the child lay dead.

*Martin Zwart*

## DER SCHATZGRÄBER

Arm am Beutel, krank am Herzen
Schleppt ich meine langen Tage.
Armut ist die größte Plage,
Reichtum ist das höchste Gut!
Und, zu enden meine Schmerzen,
Ging ich, einen Schatz zu graben.
Meine Seele sollst du haben!
Schrieb ich hin mit eignem Blut.

Und so zog ich Kreis um Kreise,
Stellte wunderbare Flammen,
Kraut und Knochenwerk zusammen:
Die Beschwörung war vollbracht.
Und auf die gelernte Weise
Grub ich nach dem alten Schatze
Auf dem angezeigten Platze;
Schwarz und stürmisch war die Nacht.

Und ich sah ein Licht von weiten,
Und es kam gleich einem Sterne
Hinten aus der fernsten Ferne,
Eben als es zwölfe schlug.
Und da galt kein Vorbereiten:
Heller wards mit einem Male
Von dem Glanz der vollen Schale,
Die ein schöner Knabe trug.

## THE SEEKER FOR TREASURE

Light of purse and heavy-hearted,
Endless days I go on dragging.
Want is like a canker nagging,
Wealth, the greatest bliss, no doubt!
And to end this state that smarted,
I set out to dig for treasure.
"Thou shalt have my soul for measure!"
With my blood I wrote it out.

Circles I delineated,
Putting wondrous flames together,
Witches' herb and bone and feather,
I performed the magic rite.
On the spot I thus located,
In the way I had been bidden,
I then dug for treasure hidden.
Dark and stormy was the night.

I beheld a radiation;
Like a star it came, yet clearer,
From the farthest distance, nearer,
Just as midnight struck nearby.
Time was not for preparation.
Of a sudden light was spreading
From the glow a bowl was shedding
That a handsome youth bore high.

Holde Augen sah ich blinken
Unter dichtem Blumenkranze;
In des Trankes Himmelsglanze
Trat er in den Kreis herein.
Und er hieß mich freundlich trinken.
Und ich dacht: es kann der Knabe
Mit der schönen lichten Gabe
Wahrlich nicht der Böse sein.

„Trinke Mut des reinen Lebens!
Dann verstehst du die Belehrung,
Kommst, mit ängstlicher Beschwörung,
Nicht zurück an diesen Ort.
Grabe hier nicht mehr vergebens.
Tages Arbeit, abends Gäste!
Saure Wochen, frohe Feste!
Sei dein künftig Zauberwort."

Locks, entwined with flowers, bordered
Lovely eyes. I saw him enter,
By the liquid glow, the center
Of the circle I had done.
"Drink," in friendly tone he ordered;
And I thought that whosoever
Brings a gift as fair, could never
Truly be the Evil-One.

"Drink the strength for living plainly!
Then you understand this lesson,
And from anxious witching session
In this place you are deterred.
Dig no more for treasure, vainly!
Work by day, at even leisure!
Sour the week, on feastdays pleasure!
Be your future magic word."

*Helen Kurz Roberts*

## DER ZAUBERLEHRLING

Hat der alte Hexenmeister
Sich doch einmal wegbegeben!
Und nun sollen seine Geister
Auch nach meinem Willen leben;
Seine Wort und Werke
Merkt ich und den Brauch,
Und mit Geistesstärke
Tu ich Wunder auch.
    Walle, walle
    Manche Strecke,
    Daß zum Zwecke
    Wasser fließe
Und mit reichem, vollem Schwalle
Zu dem Bade sich ergieße!

Und nun komm, du alter Besen!
Nimm die schlechten Lumpenhüllen!
Bist schon lange Knecht gewesen;
Nun erfülle meinen Willen!
Auf zwei Beinen stehe,
Oben sei ein Kopf,
Eile nun und gehe
Mit dem Wassertopf!
    Walle, walle
    Manche Strecke,
    Daß zum Zwecke
    Wasser fließe
Und mit reichem, vollem Schwalle
Zu dem Bade sich ergieße!

Seht, er läuft zum Ufer nieder —
Wahrlich, ist schon an dem Flusse,
Und mit Blitzesschnelle wieder
Ist er hier mit raschem Gusse.

## THE SORCERER'S APPRENTICE

He has gone the old magician
And at last I am not ridden!
Now his ghosts at my volition
Shall do just as they are bidden.
Spells I learned for hours,
Work and usage too,
By the spirit's powers
Marvels I shall do.
Wander! wander!
Find the quarter!
Draw the water!
Bring it! spill it!
And the bath, with flow from yonder,
Richly, fully surging, fill it!

Come old besom, no delaying!
Take these garments, all in tatters!
You, for long, have been obeying;
Now obey me in all matters!
Twin-legs shall support you,
Top to head shall turn,
Hurry, I exhort you,
With the water urn!
Wander! wander!
Find the quarter!
Draw the water!
Bring it! spill it!
And the bath, with flow from yonder,
Richly, fully surging, fill it!

Lo, the bank he is descending;
Truly! has now reached the river,
And like lightning, homewards wending,
Runs, more water to deliver.

Schon zum zweiten Male!
Wie das Becken schwillt!
Wie sich jede Schale
Voll mit Wasser füllt!
   Stehe! stehe!
   Denn wir haben
   Deiner Gaben
   Vollgemessen! –
Ach, ich merk' es! Wehe! wehe!
Hab' ich doch das Wort vergessen!

Ach, das Wort, worauf am Ende
Er das wird, was er gewesen!
Ach, er läuft und bringt behende!
Wärst du doch der alte Besen!
Immer neue Güsse
Bringt er schnell herein,
Ach, und hundert Flüsse
Stürzen auf mich ein!
   Nein, nicht länger
   Kann ichs lassen,
   Will ihn fassen.
   Das ist Tücke!
Ach, nun wird mir immer bänger!
Welche Miene! welche Blicke!

O, du Ausgeburt der Hölle!
Soll das ganze Haus ersaufen?
Seh ich über jede Schwelle
Doch schon Wasserströme laufen.
Ein verruchter Besen,
Der nicht hören will!
Stock, der du gewesen,
Steh doch wieder still!
   Willsts am Ende

Twice he came already!
How the basin fills!
Every cup, unsteady,
Water overspills!
Stay now! stay now!
Thou hast striven,
And hast given
Fullest measure! —
Woe! the word that I should say now
I can not recall at leisure!

Ah, the word at which, when finished,
He resumes his former figure.
Ah, he carries, undiminished!
Would, you had the broomstick's rigor!
He again delivers
Water speedily,
Ah! a hundred rivers
Tumble down on me.
My endeavor
Is to get him,
Cannot let him
Go on longer.
Ah! my fears are growing ever!
What a look! you mischiefmonger!

Oh, you fiend of Satan's keeping!
Shall the house be drowned, entire?
Over every threshold sweeping,
Streams of water join the mire.
Heinous apparition,
That is deaf at will!
Stick was your condition,
And as such, stand still!
What, I wonder,

Gar nicht lassen?
Will dich fassen,
Will dich halten
Und das alte Holz behende
Mit dem scharfen Beile spalten.

Seht, da kommt er schleppend wieder!
Wie ich mich nur auf dich werfe,
Gleich, o Kobold, liegst du nieder!
Krachend trifft die glatte Schärfe.
Wahrlich, brav getroffen!
Seht, er ist entzwei!
Und nun kann ich hoffen,
Und ich atme frei!
    Wehe! wehe!
    Beide Teile
    Stehn in Eile
    Schon als Knechte
Völlig fertig in die Höhe!
Helft mir, ach, ihr hohen Mächte!

Und sie laufen! Naß und nässer
Wirds im Saal und auf den Stufen.
Welch entsetzliches Gewässer!
Herr und Meister, hör mich rufen! –
Ach, da kommt der Meister!
Herr, die Not ist groß!
Die ich rief, die Geister,
Werd ich nun nicht los.
    ,,In die Ecke,
    Besen! Besen!
    Seids gewesen.
    Denn als Geister
Ruft euch nur zu seinem Zwecke
Erst hervor der alte Meister.''

Could appease you?
I shall seize you,
Hold you tightly,
And the dry, old wood I sunder
With this cleaver, sharpened brightly.

He comes dragging, unabated!
As I dash at you, attacking,
You, O kobold, lie prostrated,
And the sharp-edged blade falls cracking.
Well I hit him! truly!
See, he split in two!
I can breathe now duly,
And may hope anew!
Woe betide me!
Of the pieces
Neither ceases,
Each one towers
As a serf, complete, beside me!
Help me, oh, celestial powers!

There they run! The living quarters,
Hall and stairs are drowned; appalling!
Oh, how fearsome are these waters!
Lord and master! hear me calling! –
There he comes the master!
Lord, I am dismayed!
Ghosts, I called, rise faster
Than they can be laid.
"Besoms! bother
To your corner!
Be your former
Self! For vaster
Purposes, as ghosts, no other
Calls you, but the ancient master."

*Helen Kurz Roberts*

## HEIDENRÖSLEIN

Sah ein Knab' ein Röslein stehn,
Röslein auf der Heiden,
War so jung und morgenschön,
Lief er schnell, es nah zu sehn,
Sah's mit vielen Freuden.
Röslein, Röslein, Röslein rot,
Röslein auf der Heiden.

Knabe sprach: „Ich breche dich,
Röslein auf der Heiden!"
Röslein sprach: „Ich steche dich,
Daß du ewig denkst an mich,
Und ich will's nicht leiden."
Röslein, Röslein, Röslein rot,
Röslein auf der Heiden.

Und der wilde Knabe brach
's Röslein auf der Heiden;
Röslein wehrte sich und stach,
Half ihm doch kein Weh und Ach,
Mußt' es eben leiden.
Röslein, Röslein, Röslein rot,
Röslein auf der Heiden.

## ROSE AMID THE HEATHER

Saw a lad a rose one day,
Rose amid the heather,
'Twas so fresh and morning-fair
Quick he ran to see it there,
Saw it with much pleasure.
Rose, O rose, O rose so red,
Rose amid the heather.

Said the lad, "I'll pick thee then,
Rose amid the heather!"
Said the rose, "I'll prick thee then,
So thou'lt think of me again,
And I'll bear it never."
Rose, O rose, O rose so red,
Rose amid the heather.

And the wild young laddie picked
Rose amid the heather;
Rose resisted then and pricked,
Crying "Woe!" helped not a bit,
Had to bear it ever.
Rose, O rose, O rose so red,
Rose amid the heather.

*Lynda A. Marvin*

## DER GOTT UND DIE BAJADERE

Mahadöh, der Herr der Erde,
Kommt herab zum sechstenmal,
Daß er unsersgleichen werde,
Mitzufühlen Freud und Qual.
Er bequemt sich, hier zu wohnen,
Läßt sich alles selbst geschehn.
Soll er strafen oder schonen,
Muß er Menschen menschlich sehn.
Und hat er die Stadt sich als Wandrer betrachtet,
Die Großen belauert, auf Kleine geachtet,
Verläßt er sie abends, um weiterzugehn.

Als er nun hinausgegangen,
Wo die letzten Häuser sind,
Sieht er, mit gemalten Wangen,
Ein verlornes schönes Kind.
„Grüß dich, Jungfrau!" – „Dank der Ehre!
Wart, ich komme gleich hinaus." –
„Und wer bist du?" – „Bajadere,
Und dies ist der Liebe Haus."
Sie rührt sich, die Zimbeln zum Tanze zu schlagen;
Sie weiß sich so lieblich im Kreise zu tragen,
Sie neigt sich und biegt sich und reicht ihm den Strauß.

Schmeichelnd zieht sie ihn zur Schwelle,
Lebhaft ihn ins Haus hinein.
„Schöner Fremdling, lampenhelle
Soll sogleich die Hütte sein.
Bist du müd, ich will dich laben,
Lindern deiner Füße Schmerz.

## THE GOD AND THE BAYADEER

Mahadeva, great god Siva,
Has returned to earth again,
To be mortal with us mortals,
Know, as we know, joy and pain.
He agrees to dwell amongst us,
Take his lot whatever it be:
For, to punish men or spare them,
He must see men humanly.
And after the pilgrim has roamed through the city,
Has spied on the great, watched the wretched with pity,
He leaves before dark. There is much yet to see.

Reaching now the distant outskirts,
Where the rows of homes grow thin,
He perceives in gaudy raiment
A forsaken child of sin.
"Greetings, maiden." – "Sir, I thank you,
And I bid you stay and rest." –
"But who are you?" – "Bayadeer, Sir,
In this house you are love's guest."
And marking the rhythm with cymbalets ringing,
She gracefully dances through circling and swinging
And hands him the flowers she wore on her breast.

And she urges with caresses,
Bids him enter, goads him on.
"Handsome stranger, lamplit friendly
Will my cottage be anon.
You are weary. I will soothe you.
Will refresh and comfort you . . .

Was du willst, das sollst du haben,
Ruhe, Freuden oder Scherz."
Sie lindert geschäftig geheuchelte Leiden.
Der Göttliche lächelt; er siehet mit Freuden
Durch tiefes Verderben ein menschliches Herz.


Und er fordert Sklavendienste;
Immer heitrer wird sie nur,
Und des Mädchens frühe Künste
Werden nach und nach Natur.
Und so stellet auf die Blüte
Bald und bald die Frucht sich ein:
Ist Gehorsam im Gemüte,
Wird nicht fern die Liebe sein.
Aber, sie schärfer und schärfer zu prüfen,
Wählet der Kenner der Höhen und Tiefen
Lust und Entsetzen und grimmige Pein.


Und er küßt die bunten Wangen,
Und sie fühlt der Liebe Qual,
Und das Mädchen steht gefangen,
Und sie weint zum erstenmal;
Sinkt zu seinen Füßen nieder,
Nicht um Wollust noch Gewinst,
Ach, und die gelenken Glieder,
Sie versagen allen Dienst!
Und so zu des Lagers vergnüglicher Feier
Bereiten den dunklen behaglichen Schleier
Die nächtlichen Stunden, das schöne Gespinst.


Spät entschlummert unter Scherzen,
Früh erwacht nach kurzer Rast,
Findet sie an ihrem Herzen
Tot den vielgeliebten Gast.

Ask for rest, diversion, pleasure,
  All your bidding will I do."
She zealously nurses the ills he is feigning.
He cannot help smiling. With joy he sees reigning
In bawdy surroundings a heart warm and true.

He exacts a slave's performance.
  She reacts with fairer cheer:
What were skills once of her calling
  Now as nature's gifts appear.
And thus follows upon blossom
  By and by the ripened fruit.
Where obedience marks the spirit,
  Love is ready to take root.
But wishing to test her by keener devices,
He chooses, from knowledge of virtues and vices,
Delight first, then terror, and anguish to boot.

He enraptures her with kisses,
  And she tastes love's bitter core.
And she stands enthralled and weeping:
  Never did she weep before.
On her knees she falls before him,
  Not for profit nor for lust.
Oh, her limbs lost all their sinew
  Cringing helpless in the dust.
And thus, to envelop the rites of their pleasure,
Are woven the veils of the night's warming leisure
By hours of darkness, rewarding their trust.

Sleep comes late when lovers banter.
  Yet, she needs but little rest. –
In her arms lies, as she wakens,
  Dead the much-beloved guest.

Schreiend stürzt sie auf ihn nieder;
Aber nicht erweckt sie ihn,
Und man trägt die starren Glieder
Bald zur Flammengrube hin.
Sie höret die Priester, die Totengesänge,
Sie raset und rennet und teilet die Menge.
„Wer bist du? was drängt zu der Grube dich hin?"


Bei der Bahre stürzt sie nieder,
Ihr Geschrei durchdringt die Luft:
„Meinen Gatten will ich wieder!
Und ich such' ihn in der Gruft.
Soll zu Asche mir zerfallen
Dieser Glieder Götterpracht?
Mein! er war es, mein vor allen!
Ach, nur eine süße Nacht!"
Es singen die Priester: Wir tragen die Alten
Nach langem Ermatten und spätem Erkalten,
Wir tragen die Jugend, noch eh sie's gedacht.


„Höre deiner Priester Lehre:
Dieser war dein Gatte nicht.
Lebst du doch als Bajadere,
Und so hast du keine Pflicht.
Nur dem Körper folgt der Schatten
In das stille Totenreich;
Nur die Gattin folgt dem Gatten:
Das ist Pflicht und Ruhm zugleich.
Ertöne, Drommete, zu heiliger Klage!
O nehmet, ihr Götter, die Zierde der Tage,
O nehmet den Jüngling in Flammen zu euch!"


So das Chor, das ohn Erbarmen
Mehret ihres Herzens Not;

And she throws herself upon him,
But no screams can halt his flight.
And they take the lifeless body
To the flame pit's somber site.
Her ear hears the priests intoning their dirges.
And forth through the crowd in frenzy she surges. –
"Who is she?—What gives her, to be here, a right?"

By the bier she falls exhausted.
Yet her voice rings through the air:
"Give me, give me back my husband:
Death, release him from your lair. –
Shall the flames reduce to ashes
This proud body's godly sight? –
Mine he was – and no one other's –
Oh, but for one blessed night."
The priests proceed chanting: "The aged we carry
Whose flickering flame has no force left to tarry.
We carry the young, though their star shone still bright.

"Hear now, what your priests will teach you:
Husband he was not to you,
For you lead a bayadeer's life,
Owe to no one to be true.
Only shadow follows body
When it goes from where it came.
Only wife may follow husband.
That is duty; that is fame.
Let sound now the trumpet in awesome lamenting.
O gods, by your verdict which knows no relenting,
Take back your ephemeral gift in this flame."

Thus the chorus without pity
Multiplies her heart's despair.

Und mit ausgestreckten Armen
Springt sie in den heißen Tod.
Doch der Götterjüngling hebet
Aus der Flamme sich empor,
Und in seinen Armen schwebet
Die Geliebte mit hervor.
Es freut sich die Gottheit der reuigen Sünder;
Unsterbliche heben verlorene Kinder
Mit feurigen Armen zum Himmel empor.

And with outstretched arms she plunges
To her death in guttering glare.
But the beauteous god-youth rises
From the flames to realms above.
In his arms he carries with him
Bayadeer who bore him love.
The gods look with favor on penitent sinners.
They carry the wayward as ultimate winners
In fiery embraces to heavens above.

*Alexander Gode*

*Friedrich von Schiller*

### DER GRAF VON HABSBURG

Zu Aachen in seiner Kaiserpracht,
Im altertümlichen Saale,
Saß König Rudolfs heilige Macht
Beim festlichen Krönungsmahle.
Die Speisen trug der Pfalzgraf des Rheins,
Es schenkte der Böhme des perlenden Weins,
Und alle die Wähler, die sieben,
Wie der Sterne Chor um die Sonne sich stellt,
Umstanden geschäftig den Herrscher der Welt,
Die Würde des Amtes zu üben.

Und rings erfüllte den hohen Balkon
Das Volk in freud'gem Gedränge;
Laut mischte sich in der Posaunen Ton
Das jauchzende Rufen der Menge;
Denn geendigt nach langem, verderblichem Streit
War die kaiserlose, die schreckliche Zeit,
Und ein Richter war wieder auf Erden.
Nicht blind mehr waltet der eiserne Speer,
Nicht fürchtet der Schwache, der Friedliche mehr,
Des Mächtigen Beute zu werden.

Und der Kaiser ergreift den goldnen Pokal
Und spricht mit zufriedenen Blicken:
,,Wohl glänzet das Fest, wohl pranget das Mahl,
Mein königlich Herz zu entzücken;
Doch den Sänger vermiß ich, den Bringer der Lust,
Der mit süßem Klang mir bewege die Brust
Und mit göttlich erhabenen Lehren.

## THE COUNT OF HABSBURG

At Aix, in the ancient hall, bedight
In the pomp of imperial station,
There sat Rodolphus' holy might
At the feast of his coronation.
The dishes were served by the Palatine,
The king of Bohemia poured the wine,
And all the electors, the seven,
To officiate in their dignity,
Surrounded the ruler busily,
Like the stars the sun in heaven,

And, thronging the balconies all around,
The crowd, with joy and elation,
Was adding to the trumpets' sound
Loud shouts of acclamation;
For the long, the rulerless era of fright,
Was ended, after pernicious fight,
And the earth lacked a judge no longer.
No more the rule of the iron spear,
No more the weak, the peaceful need fear
Becoming a prey to the stronger.

The golden goblet the emperor seized
And spoke with contented glances:
"How splendid a meal! this brilliant feast
My royal heart entrances;
But I miss the singer, who brings delight,
To move my heart with sweet music's might
And by teachings, divinely inspired.

So hab' ich's gehalten von Jugend an,
Und was ich als Ritter gepflegt und getan,
Nicht will ich's als Kaiser entbehren."

Und sieh! In der Fürsten umgebenden Kreis
Trat der Sänger im langen Talare;
Ihm glänzte die Locke silberweiß,
Gebleicht von der Fülle der Jahre.
„Süßer Wohllaut schläft in der Saiten Gold,
Der Sänger singt von der Minne Sold,
Er preiset das Höchste, das Beste,
Was das Herz sich wünscht, was der Sinn begehrt;
Doch sage, was ist des Kaisers wert
An seinem herrlichsten Feste?"

„Nicht gebieten werd' ich dem Sänger", spricht
Der Herrscher mit lächelndem Munde,
„Er steht in des größeren Herren Pflicht,
Er gehorcht der gebietenden Stunde.
Wie in den Lüften der Sturmwind saust,
Man weiß nicht, von wannen er kommt und braust,
Wie der Quell aus verborgenen Tiefen,
So des Sängers Lied aus dem Innern schallt
Und wecket der dunkeln Gefühle Gewalt,
Die im Herzen wunderbar schliefen."

Und der Sänger rasch in die Saiten fällt
Und beginnt sie mächtig zu schlagen:
„Aufs Waidwerk hinaus ritt ein edler Held,
Den flüchtigen Gemsbock zu jagen.
Ihm folgte der Knapp mit dem Jägergeschoß,
Und als er auf seinem stattlichen Roß
In eine Au kommt geritten,
Ein Glöcklein hört er erklingen fern;

With this I have held when younger too,
And what the knight was wont to do,
Is still by the king required."

Behold! the singer stepped in the round
Of princes, his garments flowing,
With silver locks his head is crowned,
The fullness of seasons showing.
"Sweet harmonies sleep in the golden chords,
The singer sings of love's rewards,
He praises all high aspirations,
What the heart desires, the mind longs for;
Yet what could be fit for the emperor
At the greatest of celebrations?"

The ruler exclaimed with a smile: "Who commands
The singer exceeds his power,
To a greater master beholden he stands,
He obeys the compelling hour.
Like the tempest roaring in the air
And blowing, no one knows from where,
Like the spring from the deep upsweeping,
So the song of the bard from within takes its course
And rouses the dark emotions' force
That lay in the heart asleeping."

The singer then quickly struck a chord
And a mighty song resounded:
"Ahunting once went a noble lord,
The fleeting deer he hounded.
His esquire followed with quiver and bow,
And as he came to a meadow-land low,
On his stately charger riding,
He heard a bell through the morning-mist;

Ein Priester war's mit dem Leib des Herrn,
Voran kam der Mesner geschritten.

Und der Graf zur Erde sich neiget hin,
Das Haupt mit Demut entblößet,
Zu verehren mit gläubigem Christensinn,
Was alle Menschen erlöset.
Ein Bächlein aber rauschte durchs Feld,
Von des Gießbachs reißenden Fluten geschwellt,
Das hemmte der Wanderer Tritte;
Und beiseit legt jener das Sakrament,
Von den Füßen zieht er die Schuhe behend,
Damit er das Bächlein durchschritte.

‚Was schaffst du?' redet der Graf ihn an,
Der ihn verwundert betrachtet.
‚Herr, ich walle zu einem sterbenden Mann,
Der nach der Himmelskost schmachtet;
Und da ich mich nahe des Baches Steg,
Da hat ihn der strömende Gießbach hinweg
Im Strudel der Wellen gerissen.
Drum daß dem Lechzenden werde sein Heil,
So will ich das Wässerlein jetzt in Eil
Durchwaten mit nackenden Füßen.'

Da setzt ihn der Graf auf sein ritterlich Pferd
Und reicht ihm die prächtigen Zäume,
Daß er labe den Kranken, der sein begehrt,
Und die heilige Pflicht nicht versäume.
Und er selber auf seines Knappen Tier
Vergnüget noch weiter des Jagens Begier;
Der andre die Reise vollführet.
Und am nächsten Morgen, mit dankendem Blick,
Da bringt er dem Grafen sein Roß zurück,
Bescheiden am Zügel geführet.

It was a priest with the Eucharist,
In front came the sacristan striding.

"The count bared his head and bowed to the ground
With humility, most beseeming,
To revere with a Christian's faith profound,
The Saviour, all-redeeming.
But a brook that rushed through the field was swelled
By a freshet's torrential floods and held
The wanderer's step. Yet unheeding,
The latter lays down the sacrament,
Takes off the shoes from his feet, intent
On crossing the brook and proceeding.

" 'What are you doing, what is your plan?'
The count, in wonder, inquires.
'My lord, I go to a dying man
Who the food of Heaven desires;
But, approaching, I saw where a plank once lay,
The rushing torrent had swept away
The bridge in a swirling eddy.
That salvation be brought to the languishing man,
I shall wade through the brook, with what speed I can,
And I bare my feet to make ready.'

"The count lifts him up on his noble steed,
Whose saddle and reins match its beauty,
That he comfort the sick in the hour of need,
And not be remiss in his duty.
He himself takes the squire's horse in the place
Of his own and resumes the joys of the chase;
The other onward presses.
On the following morn he returns the mount,
With modesty led by the reins, to the count,
To whom his thanks he addresses.

‚Nicht wolle das Gott', rief mit Demutsinn
Der Graf, ‚daß zum Streiten und Jagen
Das Roß ich beschritte fürderhin,
Das meinen Schöpfer getragen!
Und magst du's nicht haben zu eignem Gewinst,
So bleib' es gewidmet dem göttlichen Dienst;
Denn ich hab' es *dem* ja gegeben,
Von dem ich Ehre und irdisches Gut
Zu Lehen trage und Leib und Blut
Und Seele und Atem und Leben.'

So mög' Euch Gott, der allmächtige Hort,
Der das Flehen der Schwachen erhöret,
Zu Ehren Euch bringen hier und dort,
So wie ihr jetzt ihn geehret.
Ihr seid ein mächtiger Graf, bekannt
Durch ritterlich Walten im Schweizerland;
Euch blühn sechs liebliche Töchter.
So mögen sie', rief er begeistert aus,
‚Sechs Kronen Euch bringen in Euer Haus
Und glänzen die spätsten Geschlechter!' "

Und mit sinnendem Haupt saß der Kaiser da,
Als dächt' er vergangener Zeiten;
Jetzt, da er dem Sänger ins Auge sah,
Da ergreift ihn der Worte Bedeuten.
Die Züge des Priesters erkennt er schnell
Und verbirgt der Tränen stürzenden Quell
In des Mantels purpurnen Falten.
Und alles blickte den Kaiser an
Und erkannte den Grafen, der das getan,
Und verehrte das göttliche Walten.

" 'May God forbid,' the nobleman cried,
Who was humble of mind and behavior,
'That for warring and hunting I ever should ride
A horse that has borne my Saviour!
And should you not want it yourself and refuse,
I dedicate it to sacred use;
For I gave it to him who allowed me
To hold great honors and wealth on earth,
Who made my body and blood, who at birth
With soul and life has endowed me.'

" 'Then God, the Almighty, who does respond
To the pleas of the humble, may aid you
To gain high honors on earth and beyond,
As you honored Him who made you.
In Switzerland you are known to be
A knight of might and chivalry,
Six maidens fair call you father.
'May each,' he exclaimed, 'find a royal spouse,
To bring six crowns into your house
And glory your line ever gather!' "

But the emperor's thoughts were lost in the past,
His eyes he was pensively screening;
But now, that he looked at the singer at last,
He was gripped by the words' true meaning.
The face of the priest in the bard he beholds
And hides in his mantle's purple folds
The tears that brook no retention.
To the emperor turned the eyes of the throng,
They recognized, all, the count of the song
And revered the divine intervention.

*Helen Kurz Roberts*

## DIE KRANICHE DES IBYKUS

Zum Kampf der Wagen und Gesänge,
Der auf Korinthus' Landesenge
Der Griechen Stämme froh vereint,
Zog Ibykus, der Götterfreund.
Ihm schenkte des Gesanges Gabe,
Der Lieder süßen Mund Apoll;
So wandert' er, an leichtem Stabe,
Aus Rhegium, des Gottes voll.

Schon winkt auf hohem Bergesrücken
Akrokorinth des Wandrers Blicken,
Und in Poseidons Fichtenhain
Tritt er mit frommem Schauder ein.
Nichts regt sich um ihn her; nur Schwärme
Von Kranichen begleiten ihn,
Die fernhin nach des Südens Wärme
In graulichtem Geschwader ziehn.

„Seid mir gegrüßt, befreundte Scharen,
Die mir zur See Begleiter waren!
Zum guten Zeichen nehm' ich euch,
Mein Los, es ist dem euren gleich:
Von fernher kommen wir gezogen
Und flehen um ein wirtlich Dach.
Sei uns der Gastliche gewogen,
Der von dem Fremdling wehrt die Schmach!"

Und munter fördert er die Schritte
Und sieht sich in des Waldes Mitte –
Da sperren, auf gedrangem Steg,
Zwei Mörder plötzlich seinen Weg.
Zum Kampfe muß er sich bereiten,
Doch bald ermattet sinkt die Hand,

## THE CRANES OF IBYCUS

To strife of chariots and songs,
That joy-united Grecian throngs
On Corinth's isthmus-land attend,
Went Ibycus, the god's own friend.
To him had fair Apollo granted
Two lips all sweet with song and lay;
On light staff leaning, god-enchanted,
From Rhegium forth he made his way.

Acrocorinth, on mountain risen,
Already greets the wand'rer's vision,
And he begins, with pious dread,
Poseidon's grove of firs to tread.
Naught stirs all round him save a swarm
Of cranes, who share his wand'rer's way,
Who far to regions south and warm
Wing on and on in squadron gray.

"O friendly hosts, all hail to ye
Who shared my sail across the sea!
I deem ye as a fav'ring sign,
Your destiny's akin to mine:
From lands afar we wand'rers stray
And pray for some kind shelt'ring-place.
May Zeus-protector guide our way,
Who guards the stranger from disgrace!"

And carefree he the wood doth enter
And reaches soon the dark grove's center –
There, on a narrow bridge, by force
Two murd'rers sudden bar his course.
For mortal strife he must make ready,
But soon his wearied hand sinks low;

Sie hat der Leier zarte Saiten,
Doch nie des Bogens Kraft gespannt.

Er ruft die Menschen an, die Götter,
Sein Flehen dringt zu keinem Retter;
Wie weit er auch die Stimme schickt,
Nichts Lebendes wird hier erblickt.
„So muß ich hier verlassen sterben,
Auf fremdem Boden, unbeweint,
Durch böser Buben Hand verderben,
Wo auch kein Rächer mir erscheint!"

Und schwer getroffen sinkt er nieder,
Da rauscht der Kraniche Gefieder;
Er hört, schon kann er nicht mehr sehn,
Die nahen Stimmen furchtbar krähn.
„Von euch, ihr Kraniche dort oben,
Wenn keine andre Stimme spricht,
Sei meines Mordes Klag erhoben!"
Er ruft es, und sein Auge bricht.

Der nackte Leichnam wird gefunden,
Und bald, obgleich entstellt von Wunden,
Erkennt der Gastfreund in Korinth
Die Züge, die ihm teuer sind.
„Und muß ich so dich wiederfinden,
Und hoffte, mit der Fichte Kranz
Des Sängers Schläfe zu umwinden,
Bestrahlt von seines Ruhmes Glanz!"

Und jammernd hörens alle Gäste,
Versammelt bei Poseidons Feste,
Ganz Griechenland ergreift der Schmerz,
Verloren hat ihn jedes Herz.
Und stürmend drängt sich zum Prytanen

For gentle lyre-strings 'twas steady,
It ne'er had strung the deadly bow.

To men, to gods he pleads entreaty,
His prayer finds no savior's pity,
However far his voice he sends,
Naught living to his cry attends.
"Then must I perish here forsaken,
On foreign soil, unmourned and still,
My life by churlish fellows taken,
No one my vengeance to fulfill!"

And stricken deep he sinks, eyes blurring,
When, lo! the wings of cranes come whirring,
He hears – though he no more can see –
Their slender throats screech fearfully.
"By you, O cranes, there over me,
If no one else the utt'rance make,
Be borne to man my murder plea!"
He speaks it, and his dim eyes break.

Ere long the naked corpse is found,
And though defaced by many a wound,
His host in Corinth swift can tell
Those features that he loved so well:
"And is it thus that I must find thee,
And I had hoped with poet-crown,
With gentle spruce-wreath to entwine thee,
Illumined by thy bright renown!"

And one great sigh of sad lamenting
Shakes all Poseidon's feast attending.
All Greece is torn by sorrow's smart,
His loss burns deep in every heart;
The people throng in raging seas

Das Volk, es fordert seine Wut,
Zu rächen des Erschlagnen Manen,
Zu sühnen mit des Mörders Blut.


Doch wo die Spur, die aus der Menge,
Der Völker flutendem Gedränge,
Gelocket von der Spiele Pracht,
Den schwarzen Täter kenntlich macht?
Sinds Räuber, die ihn feig erschlagen?
Tats neidisch ein verborgner Feind?
Nur Helios vermags zu sagen,
Der alles Irdische bescheint.


Er geht vielleicht mit frechem Schritte
Jetzt eben durch der Griechen Mitte,
Und während ihn die Rache sucht,
Genießt er seines Frevels Frucht.
Auf ihres eignen Tempels Schwelle
Trotzt er vielleicht den Göttern, mengt
Sich dreist in jene Menschenwelle,
Die dort sich zum Theater drängt.


Denn Bank an Bank gedränget sitzen,
Es brechen fast der Bühne Stützen,
Herbeigeströmt von fern und nah,
Der Griechen Völker wartend da.
Dumpfbrausend wie des Meeres Wogen,
Von Menschen wimmelnd wächst der Bau
In weiter stets geschweiftem Bogen
Hinauf bis in des Himmels Blau.


Wer zählt die Völker, nennt die Namen,
Die gastlich hier zusammen kamen?
Von Theseus' Stadt, von Aulis' Strand,
Von Phocis, vom Spartanerland,

Before their judge, his wrath to urge,
The slain man's manes to appease,
With murd'rer's blood his death to purge.

But where's the trace that from the surging
Of undulating peoples merging,
Allured by sportive glories bright,
Shall bring the murd'rer back to light?
Did robbers craven make the kill?
Was't envy of some secret foe?
That Helios alone can tell,
Whose rays illume all things below.

E'en now, perchance, with saunter shameless
He walks the Grecian crowd, still blameless –
Whilst vengeance follows in pursuit,
He gloats o'er his transgression's fruit;
The very gods perchance he braves
Upon the threshold of their fane –
Joins boldly in the human waves
That surge yon theater to gain.

For gathered there from far and near,
Close-packed on benches, tier on tier,
The tribes of Greece sit waiting all –
The burdened stage bids fair to fall;
Deep rumbling, full – as sea-surf roars,
The teeming arch, a human sea,
In ever-widening span upsoars
Into the sky's blue canopy.

Who knows the nation, who the name
Of all who here together came?
From Theseus' town, from Aulis' strand,
From Phocis, from the Spartans' land,

Von Asiens entlegner Küste,
Von allen Inseln kamen sie
Und horchen von dem Schaugerüste
Des Chores grauser Melodie,

Der streng und ernst, nach alter Sitte,
Mit langsam abgemeßnem Schritte
Hervortritt aus dem Hintergrund,
Umwandelnd des Theaters Rund.
So schreiten keine ird'schen Weiber,
Die zeugete kein sterblich Haus!
Es steigt das Riesenmaß der Leiber
Hoch über menschliches hinaus.

Ein schwarzer Mantel schlägt die Lenden,
Sie schwingen in entfleischten Händen
Der Fackel düsterrote Glut,
In ihren Wangen fließt kein Blut;
Und wo die Haare lieblich flattern,
Um Menschenstirnen freundlich wehn,
Da sieht man Schlangen hier und Nattern
Die giftgeschwollnen Bäuche blähn.

Und schauerlich, gedreht im Kreise,
Beginnen sie des Hymnus Weise,
Der durch das Herz zerreißend dringt,
Die Bande um den Frevler schlingt.
Besinnungraubend, herzbetörend
Schallt der Erinnyen Gesang,
Er schallt, des Hörers Mark verzehrend,
Und duldet nicht der Leier Klang:

„Wohl dem, der frei von Schuld und Fehle
Bewahrt die kindlich reine Seele!
Ihm dürfen wir nicht rächend nahn,

Yea, e'en from Asia's coast far distant,
From every island they did throng,
And now, by yonder show-stage, listened
To Grecian chorus' gruesome song.

Severe and stern in custom treasured,
With stolid steps sedate and measured
It marches forth from background dark,
And circles round the theater's arc.
That stride is not of women mortal,
No earthly race gave birth to them!
Their giant forms tower up transportal
High o'er the puny sons of men.

About their thighs black cloaks hang clinging,
Their fleshless hands are steadfast swinging
Dull torches of half-hidden glow,
While in their cheeks no blood dares flow;
And there where lovely locks loose flutter
Right friendly round a mortal brow,
Here one sees snakes and vipers clutter,
Their bodies poison-swelled enow.

And in a fearful circle rounded,
The dread and awesome song is sounded,
That rending fills each heart with fear,
And locks the sinner in its sphere.
To dim the senses, hearts to harrow,
Echoes the furies' fateful chant,
Resounds, devours the listener's marrow,
Permits no lyres' accompaniment:

"Yea, happy he who's free of error!
On him we dare not wreak our terror.
Who keeps his soul childlike and pure,

Er wandelt frei des Lebens Bahn.
Doch wehe, wehe, wer verstohlen
Des Mordes schwere Tat vollbracht!
Wir heften uns an seine Sohlen,
Das furchtbare Geschlecht der Nacht.

Und glaubt er fliehend zu entspringen,
Geflügelt sind wir da, die Schlingen
Ihm werfend um den flücht'gen Fuß,
Daß er zu Boden fallen muß.
So jagen wir ihn, ohn Ermatten,
Versöhnen kann uns keine Reu,
Ihn fort und fort bis zu den Schatten
Und geben ihn auch dort nicht frei."

So singend tanzen sie den Reigen,
Und Stille, wie des Todes Schweigen,
Liegt überm ganzen Hause schwer,
Als ob die Gottheit nahe wär.
Und feierlich, nach alter Sitte,
Umwandelnd des Theaters Rund,
Mit langsam abgemeßnem Schritte
Verschwinden sie im Hintergrund.

Und zwischen Trug und Wahrheit schwebet
Noch zweifelnd jede Brust und bebet
Und huldiget der furchtbar'n Macht,
Die richtend im Verborgnen wacht,
Die unerforschlich, unergründet
Des Schicksals dunkeln Knäuel flicht,
Dem tiefen Herzen sich verkündet,
Doch fliehet vor dem Sonnenlicht.

Da hört man auf den höchsten Stufen
Auf einmal eine Stimme rufen:

Traverses life wrath-free and sure.
But woe to him, who dark and hidden
Hath done the deed of murder base!
We fasten on his steps unbidden,
Dark night's avenging, awful race.

"And if he thinks to 'scape by fleeing,
On wings we come, our nets all-seeing
About his fleeting feet we cast,
So that he needs must fall at last.
Thus do we hunt him, tiring never,
Repentance vain we never heed,
Straight on e'en to the shades' own river,
And even there he is not freed."

Thus on they dance and chant in chillness,
And silence, like unto death's stillness,
Lies heavy over house and sky
As if the deity were nigh.
And solemnly, in custom treasured,
Encircling all the theater's arc,
With stolid step sedate and measured
They vanish in the background dark.

And twixt deceit and truth still wavers
Each human doubting breast, and quavers,
And homage pays to that dread might
That judging watches, hid from sight,
That, fathomless and unexposed,
Entwines the obscure skein of fate;
In bosom depths it is disclosed,
Howe'er it flees from sunlight's hate.

Then sudden from the tier most high
A voice is heard by all to cry:

„Sieh da! sieh da, Timotheus,
Die Kraniche des Ibykus!"
Und finster plötzlich wird der Himmel,
Und über dem Theater hin
Sieht man, in schwärzlichem Gewimmel,
Ein Kranichheer vorüberziehn.

„Des Ibykus!" – Der teure Name
Rührt jede Brust mit neuem Grame,
Und wie im Meere Well auf Well,
So läufts von Mund zu Munde schnell:
„Des Ibykus? den wir beweinen?
Den eine Mörderhand erschlug?
Was ists mit dem? was kann er meinen?
Was ists mit diesem Kranichzug?" –

Und lauter immer wird die Frage,
Und ahnend fliegts mit Blitzesschlage
Durch alle Herzen: „Gebet acht,
Das ist der Eumeniden Macht!
Der fromme Dichter wird gerochen,
Der Mörder bietet selbst sich dar –
Ergreift ihn, der das Wort gesprochen,
Und ihn, an den's gerichtet war!"

Doch dem war kaum das Wort entfahren,
Möcht ers im Busen gern bewahren;
Umsonst! Der schreckenbleiche Mund
Macht schnell die Schuldbewußten kund.
Man reißt und schleppt sie vor den
Die Szene wird zum Tribunal, [Richter,
Und es gestehn die Bösewichter,
Getroffen von der Rache Strahl.

"See there, see there, Timotheus!
The cranes, the cranes of Ibycus!"
And swift a darkness dims the heaven,
And o'er the theater and away
One sees in teeming swarm of ebon
A troop of cranes wing on its way.

"Of Ibycus!" – That name so treasured
Moves every breast with grief fresh-measured –
As waves on waves in oceans rise,
From mouth to mouth it swiftly flies:
"Of Ibycus, whom we are mourning,
Who fell for fiendish murd'rers' gains?
What is't with him? What means his warning?
And what imports this swarm of cranes?"

And louder ever grow the cries,
With lightning-speed foreboding flies
Through every heart: "'Tis clear as light,
This is th' avenging furies' might!
The poet's manes are appeased,
The murd'rer seeks his own arrest!
Let him who spoke the word be seized,
And him to whom it was addressed."

That word he had no sooner uttered,
Than he had fain his bosom fettered –
In vain! Mouths pale with terror's hue
Full swift reveal the guilty two.
Before the judge they're dragged in passion,
A jury gathers at his call,
And both the culprits make confession,
As 'neath the vengeance-stroke they fall.

*Harold Lenz*

## DAS SIEGESFEST

Priams Feste war gesunken,
Troja lag in Schutt und Staub,
Und die Griechen, siegestrunken,
Reich beladen mit dem Raub,
Saßen auf den hohen Schiffen
Längs des Hellespontos Strand,
Auf der frohen Fahrt begriffen
Nach dem schönen Griechenland.
    Stimmet an die frohen Lieder!
    Denn dem väterlichen Herd
    Sind die Schiffe zugekehrt,
    Und zur Heimat geht es wieder.

Und in langen Reihen, klagend,
Saß der Trojerinnen Schar,
Schmerzvoll an die Brüste schlagend,
Bleich, mit aufgelöstem Haar.
In das wilde Fest der Freuden
Mischten sie den Wehgesang,
Weinend um das eigne Leiden
In des Reiches Untergang.
    Lebe wohl, geliebter Boden!
    Von der süßen Heimat fern
    Folgen wir dem fremden Herrn.
    Ach wie glücklich sind die Toten!

Und den hohen Göttern zündet
Kalchas jetzt das Opfer an;
Pallas, die die Städte gründet
Und zertrümmert, ruft er an
Und Neptun, der um die Länder
Seinen Wogengürtel schlingt,
Und den Zeus, den Schreckensender,

## THE FEAST OF VICTORY

Troy in ruins, devastated!
Priam's stronghold, – level soil!
And the Greeks, with triumph sated,
Richly laden with the spoil,
Sat on high-prowed vessels, faring
By the Hellespontos' strand,
On their joyous voyage bearing
Towards the fair Hellenic land.
   Gaily sing in celebration!
   To the hearth paternal now
   Pointing is the vessels prow,
   With sweet home for destination.

But in endless lines, lamenting,
Sat the Trojan women there,
Beat their breasts, their sorrow venting,
Pale, with loose, dishevelled hair.
To the feast of wild rejoicing
They admixed their threnody,
Anguish for their own fate voicing,
For their country's destiny.
   Fare thou well, O soil I cherished!
   We so far from home adored,
   Follow now a foreign lord.
   Fortunate are those that perished!

Calchas offered gifts and praises
To the Gods, the incense smoked.
Pallas, she who builds and razes
Mighty cities, was invoked.
Also Neptune, who is ringing
With his wave-belt all the lands,
Zeus, the gruesome Aegis swinging,

Der die Ägis grausend schwingt.
Ausgestritten, ausgerungen
Ist der lange, schwere Streit,
Ausgefüllt der Kreis der Zeit,
Und die große Stadt bezwungen.

Atreus' Sohn, der Fürst der Scharen,
Übersah der Völker Zahl,
Die mit ihm gezogen waren
Einst in des Skamanders Tal.
Und des Kummers finstre Wolke
Zog sich um des Königs Blick:
Von dem hergeführten Volke
Bracht er wen'ge nur zurück.
　　Drum erhebe frohe Lieder,
　　Wer die Heimat wiedersieht,
　　Wem noch frisch das Leben blüht!
　　Denn nicht alle kehren wieder.

,,Alle nicht, die wiederkehren,
Mögen sich des Heimzugs freun,
An den häuslichen Altären
Kann der Mord bereitet sein.
Mancher fiel durch Freundestücke,
Den die blut'ge Schlacht verfehlt!"
Sprachs Ulyß mit Warnungsblicke,
Von Athenens Geist beseelt.
　　Glücklich, wem der Gattin Treue
　　Rein und keusch das Haus bewahrt!
　　Denn das Weib ist falscher Art,
　　Und die Arge liebt das Neue.

Und des frisch erkämpften Weibes
Freut sich der Atrid und strickt
Um den Reiz des schönen Leibes

He who thunderbolts commands.
 Fought, wrought out is now the heated
 Contest, long and yet sublime,
 Filled the cycle of the time
 And the haughty town defeated.

Atreus' son, the hosts' commander,
Then reviewed the nations all
That had sailed for the Skamander,
Following their leader's call.
And the king's regard was shrouded
By a cloud of deep concern;
Of his ranks, ah! once so crowded,
Few are those that now return.
 Sing ye paeans in communion
 Those who'll see the fatherland,
 Who still life and youth command!
 Not for all will be reunion.

"Yet not all who are returning
Can expect a happy fate;
Where the altar brand is burning
Murder foul may lie in wait.
Whom the bloody battle misses
He may die, by friends betrayed!"
Spake, with warning glance, Ulysses
By Athene's spirit swayed.
 Blest whose home a wife arranges
 Faithful, chaste, who never strays!
 Fickle are most women's ways
 And the wily favor changes.

In the woman, just acquired,
Now rejoices the Atride,
Takes her body, much desired,

Seine Arme hochbeglückt.
„Böses Werk muß untergehen,
Rache folgt der Freveltat;
Denn gerecht in Himmelshöhen
Waltet des Kroniden Rat."
   Böses muß mit Bösem enden;
   An dem frevelnden Geschlecht
   Rächet Zeus das Gastesrecht,
   Wägend mit gerechten Händen.

„Wohl dem Glücklichen mags ziemen,"
Ruft Oïleus' tapfrer Sohn,
„Die Regierenden zu rühmen
Auf dem hohen Himmelsthron!
Ohne Wahl verteilt die Gaben,
Ohne Billigkeit das Glück;
Denn Patroklus liegt begraben,
Und Thersites kommt zurück!"
   Weil das Glück aus seiner Tonnen
   Die Geschicke blind verstreut,
   Freue sich und jauchze heut,
   Wer das Lebenslos gewonnen!

„Ja, der Krieg verschlingt die Besten!
Ewig werde dein gedacht,
Bruder, bei der Griechen Festen,
Der ein Turm war in der Schlacht.
Da der Griechen Schiffe brannten,
War in deinem Arm das Heil;
Doch dem Schlauen, Vielgewandten
Ward der schöne Preis zuteil."
   Friede deinen heil'gen Resten!
   Nicht der Feind hat dich entrafft:
   Ajax fiel durch Ajax' Kraft.
   Ach, der Zorn verderbt die Besten!

In his arms with joy and pride.
Wicked deed has no duration,
Vengeance follows evil done.
High in his celestial station
Rules in justice Kronos' son.
    "Evil takes an evil ending;
    Outraged hospitality,
    Zeus, librating equity,
    Venges on the house offending."

"One, who knows but happy hours,"
Calls Oïleus' son with heat,
"It befits to praise the powers
On their high Olympian seat!
Luck, unjust and undiscerning,
Showers gifts on fool and knave.
Lo! Thersites is returning,
But Patroclus in his grave!"
    Thus, as Luck is blindly giving,
    Drawing from her ton our fate,
    Let rejoice and jubilate
    Those who won the prize of living!

"Yea, the best the wars devour,
Brother, Greeks will think of thee
Who in battle wast a tower,
Praise, at feasts, thy gallantry.
When the Grecian ships were fired,
Their salvation was thy arm;
Yet the sly, the ruse-inspired,
Won the prize and gained the palm."
    May thy shades sweet peace acquire!
    Thee, no foe did ever smite!
    Ajax fell through Ajax' might.
    Ah, the best are wrecked by ire!

Dem Erzeuger jetzt, dem großen,
Gießt Neoptolem des Weins:
„Unter allen ird'schen Losen,
Hoher Vater, preis ich deins:
Von des Lebens Gütern allen
Ist der Ruhm das höchste doch;
Wenn der Leib in Staub zerfallen,
Lebt der große Name noch."
   Tapfrer, deines Ruhmes Schimmer
   Wird unsterblich sein im Lied;
   Denn das ird'sche Leben flieht,
   Und die Toten dauern immer.


„Weil des Liedes Stimmen schweigen
Von dem überwundnen Mann,
So will ich für Hektorn zeugen",
Hub der Sohn des Tydeus an;
„Der für seine Hausaltäre
Kämpfend, ein Beschirmer, fiel –
Krönt den Sieger größre Ehre,
Ehret ihn das schönre Ziel!"
   Der für seine Hausaltäre
   Kämpfend sank, ein Schirm und Hort,
   Auch in Feindes Munde fort
   Lebt ihm seines Namens Ehre.


Nestor jetzt, der alte Zecher,
Der drei Menschenalter sah,
Reicht den laubumkränzten Becher
Der betränten Hekuba:
„Trink ihn aus, den Trank der Labe,
Und vergiß den großen Schmerz!
Wundervoll ist Bacchus' Gabe,
Balsam fürs zerrißne Herz."
   Trink ihn aus, den Trank der Labe,

Now unto his great begetter
Neoptolem pours the wine.
"Noble father, never better
Earthly lot there was than thine!
Of the goods, for which we fumble
In this life, the best is fame!
When the flesh to dust must crumble,
Lives the greatness of a name!"
 Glory's luster fadeth never;
 Thou immortal art in song;
 Life on earth may not be long,
 But the dead will last for ever.

"If the song neglects to mention
Him, the brave though vanquished man,
I to Hector draw attention,"
Tydeus' son, he thus began;
"He who fell in combat gory,
Fighting for his altar's flame —
Though the victor's is the glory,
Him does glorify the aim!"
 He who died, the shield, defender,
 For his altar's sacred flame,
 Highest honors to his name
 Even enemy lips must render.

"Old king Nestor, drinker, rover,
He of ten and fourscore years,
Took the vine-wreathed chalice over
To Queen Hecuba, in tears.
"Drain the cup of consolation
And forget thy poignant smart!
Sweet is Bacchus' great donation,
Balm unto a pain-torn heart."
 Drain the cup of consolation

Und vergiß den großen Schmerz!
Balsam fürs zerrißne Herz,
Wundervoll ist Bacchus' Gabe.

„Denn auch Niobe, dem schweren
Zorn der Himmlischen ein Ziel,
Kostete die Frucht der Ähren
Und bezwang das Schmerzgefühl.
Denn so lang die Lebensquelle
Schäumet an der Lippen Rand,
Ist der Schmerz in Lethes Welle
Tief versenkt und festgebannt!"
　　Denn so lang die Lebensquelle
　　An der Lippen Rande schäumt,
　　Ist der Jammer weggeträumt,
　　Fortgespült in Lethes Welle.

Und von ihrem Gott ergriffen,
Hub sich jetzt die Seherin,
Blickte von den hohen Schiffen
Nach dem Rauch der Heimat hin.
„Rauch ist alles ird'sche Wesen;
Wie des Dampfes Säule weht,
Schwinden alle Erdengrößen;
Nur die Götter bleiben stet."
　　Um das Roß des Reiters schweben,
　　Um das Schiff die Sorgen her;
　　Morgen können wir's nicht mehr,
　　Darum laßt uns heute leben!

And forget thy poignant smart!
Balm unto the pain-torn heart,
Sweet is Bacchus' great donation!

"When, the butt of Heaven's ire,
Niobe was all in tears,
She restrained her feelings dire,
Tasting of the fruit of ears.
For as long as life's spring bubbles,
Foaming wets the lips that thirst,
Charmed away are pains and troubles,
Deep in Lethe's waves immersed!"
     For as long as life's spring bubbles,
     Wets with foam the thirsting lips,
     Pain is dreamed away and slips
     To where Lethe drowns all troubles.

"Then the prophetess, inspired
By her god, rose up to gaze
From the ships at Troy, the fired,
At the smoke above the blaze.
"Smoke is all the earthly essence!
Like the wind-blown smoke must fade
Earthly greatness! Evanescence
All! The Gods alone are staid."
     Over horse and rider sorrow
     Hovers, o'er the vessel's spray.
     Gaily let us live today,
     Death may claim us on the morrow!

                              *Helen Kurz Roberts*

## KASSANDRA

Freude war in Trojas Hallen,
Eh die hohe Feste fiel;
Jubelhymnen hört man schallen
In der Saiten goldnes Spiel;
Alle Hände ruhen müde
Von dem tränenvollen Streit,
Weil der herrliche Pelide
Priams schöne Tochter freit.

Und geschmückt mit Lorbeerreisern,
Festlich wallet Schar auf Schar
Nach der Götter heil'gen Häusern,
Zu des Thymbriers Altar.
Dumpf erbrausend durch die Gassen
Wälzt sich die bacchant'sche Lust,
Und in ihrem Schmerz verlassen
War nur eine traur'ge Brust.

Freudlos in der Freude Fülle,
Ungesellig und allein,
Wandelte Kassandra stille
In Apollos Lorbeerhain.
In des Waldes tiefste Gründe
Flüchtete die Seherin,
Und sie warf die Priesterbinde
Zu der Erde zürnend hin:

,,Alles ist der Freude offen,
Alle Herzen sind beglückt,
Und die alten Eltern hoffen,
Und die Schwester steht geschmückt.
Ich allein muß einsam trauern,
Denn mich flieht der süße Wahn,
Und geflügelt diesen Mauern
Seh ich das Verderben nahn.

## CASSANDRA

Joy in Troy's vast halls abounded
Ere the noble stronghold fell.
Hymns of jubilation sounded
To the lyre's golden spell.
Weary of the fearful slaughter
Resting are all hands at ease,
For King Priam's fairest daughter
Weds the splendid Achilles.

Laurel-crowned, with festive faces
Pass the crowds in endless line
Heading for the holy places,
For Apollo's sacred shrine.
And bacchantic joy does waken
Roaring, tears through street and mart;
In her sorrow, quite forsaken
Was but one despairing heart.

Joyless there, where joy abounded,
Friendless and misunderstood,
Walked Cassandra, fear-surrounded,
In Apollo's laurel wood.
In the forest's deep recesses
Refuge sought the prophetess,
Cast the priest-band from her tresses
To the ground with bitterness.

"All the gates to joy are oping,
All the hearts are gay and light
And my aged parents hoping
And my sister stands bedight.
I alone must walk in sorrow,
Sweet illusion flees from me,
To these walls I see the morrow
Bringing death and agony.

Eine Fackel seh ich glühen,
Aber nicht in Hymens Hand;
Nach den Wolken seh ichs ziehen,
Aber nicht wie Opferbrand.
Feste seh ich froh bereiten,
Doch im ahnungsvollen Geist
Hör ich schon des Gottes Schreiten,
Der sie jammervoll zerreißt.

Und sie schelten meine Klagen,
Und sie höhnen meinen Schmerz,
Einsam in die Wüste tragen
Muß ich mein gequältes Herz,
Von den Glücklichen gemieden,
Und den Fröhlichen ein Spott!
Schweres hast du mir beschieden,
Pythischer, du arger Gott!

Dein Orakel zu verkünden,
Warum warfest du mich hin
In die Stadt der ewig Blinden,
Mit dem aufgeschloßnen Sinn?
Warum gabst du mir zu sehen,
Was ich doch nicht wenden kann?
Das Verhängte muß geschehen,
Das Gefürchtete muß nahn.

Frommts, den Schleier aufzuheben,
Wo das nahe Schrecknis droht?
Nur der Irrtum ist das Leben,
Und das Wissen ist der Tod.
Nimm, o nimm die traur'ge Klarheit,
Mir vom Aug den blut'gen Schein!
Schrecklich ist es, deiner Wahrheit
Sterbliches Gefäß zu sein.

"And a torch I see it flaring,
But 'tis not in Hymen's hand.
To the clouds the smoke is bearing,
But 'tis not the altar's brand.
Feasts they are preparing, gaily,
Yet my mind's acuity
Hears the god approaching daily
Who destroys them woefully.

"Ah, they scold my lamentations
And deride my deepest smart,
Lonesome into desolation
I must take my tortured heart,
And I know the happy shun me,
Bear the gay ones' mockery!
See the wrong that thou hast done me,
Pythian, god of cruelty!

"To announce how thou art minded,
I was chosen. Yet why take,
To this town of ever-blinded,
One with mind so wide-awake?
Why foresee when I can never
Alter what the gods decree?
What is feared is nearing, ever,
What is fated, that will be.

"Of what use to have misgiving
Ere one feels perdition's breath?
Only error meaneth living
But all insight meaneth death.
Take away my divinations
From my eyes the blood-red sheen!
Woe to me, thy revelations'
Mortal vessel I have been.

Meine Blindheit gib mir wieder
Und den fröhlich dunkeln Sinn!
Nimmer sang ich freud'ge Lieder,
Seit ich deine Stimme bin.
Zukunft hast du mir gegeben,
Doch du nahmst den Augenblick,
Nahmst der Stunde fröhlich Leben –
Nimm dein falsch Geschenk zurück!

Nimmer mit dem Schmuck der Bräute
Kränzt ich mir das duft'ge Haar,
Seit ich deinem Dienst mich weihte
An dem traurigen Altar.
Meine Jugend war nur Weinen,
Und ich kannte nur den Schmerz,
Jede herbe Not der Meinen
Schlug an mein empfindend Herz.

Fröhlich seh ich die Gespielen,
Alles um mich lebt und liebt
In der Jugend Lustgefühlen,
Mir nur ist das Herz getrübt.
Mir erscheint der Lenz vergebens,
Der die Erde festlich schmückt:
Wer erfreute sich des Lebens,
Der in seine Tiefen blickt!

Selig preis ich Polyxenen
In des Herzens trunknem Wahn,
Denn den Besten der Hellenen
Hofft sie bräutlich zu umfahn.
Stolz ist ihre Brust gehoben,
Ihre Wonne faßt sie kaum,
Nicht euch Himmlische dort oben
Neidet sie in ihrem Traum.

"Blind my mental eye, admeasure
Ignorance that can rejoice!
Never have I sung for pleasure
Since I have become thy voice.
Future thou art freely giving,
But the moment didst retain
And the hour's joyous living.
Take thy gift that I disdain.

"Never with a bride's attire
Did I crown my festive hair
Since I vowed myself, entire,
At thy altar of despair;
And my youth has been but weeping
And I knew but bitter smart,
All my people's woes were seeping
Into my receptive heart.

"Joy is everywhere appealing,
All around me love and live,
And to youth's exalted feeling
I must be insensitive.
Naught avails me spring's endeavor
That endows the earth with bliss.
Who can savor life who ever
Has looked down in its abyss?

"Polyxena I must envy
In her heart's deluded bliss,
For she hopes the noblest enemy
Will receive her bridal kiss.
And her eye is filled with wonder
And her breast with pride supreme.
Not the deities up yonder
Would she envy in her dream.

Und auch ich hab ihn gesehen,
Den das Herz verlangend wählt,
Seine schönen Blicke flehen,
Von der Liebe Glut beseelt.
Gerne möcht ich mit dem Gatten
In die heim'sche Wohnung ziehn,
Doch es tritt ein styg'scher Schatten
Nächtlich zwischen mich und ihn.

Ihre bleichen Larven alle
Sendet mir Proserpina;
Wo ich wandre, wo ich walle,
Stehen mir die Geister da.
In der Jugend frohe Spiele
Drängen sie sich grausend ein,
Ein entsetzliches Gewühle –
Nimmer kann ich fröhlich sein.

Und den Mordstahl seh ich blinken
Und das Mörderauge glühn;
Nicht zur Rechten, nicht zur Linken
Kann ich vor dem Schrecknis fliehn;
Nicht die Blicke darf ich wenden;
Wissend, schauend, unverwandt
Muß ich mein Geschick vollenden,
Fallend in dem fremden Land."

Und noch hallen ihre Worte –
Horch! da dringt verworrner Ton
Fernher aus des Tempels Pforte:
Tot lag Thetis' großer Sohn!
Eris schüttelt ihre Schlangen,
Alle Götter fliehn davon,
Und des Donners Wolken hangen
Schwer herab auf Ilion.

"Also I saw him I heeded,
Whom I long for, all above.
And his soulful eyes have pleaded,
Glowing with the light of love.
How I wish that I could rightly
Have a home's felicity,
But a Stygian shadow nightly
Steps between my love and me.

"Pallid phantoms from down yonder,
Proserpina sends in hosts;
Where I walk and where I wander,
Always I shall meet her ghosts.
In our innocent enjoyments
Thrust they their ubiquity.
Oh the horrible embroilment!
Happy I can never be.

"And the murd'rous steel is gleaming
And the murder-eye aglow;
Right or left, whatever scheming,
I cannot ward off the blow;
Nor avert my eyes descrying;
Knowing, seeing, steadfastly,
In a foreign country dying,
I fulfill my destiny."

And her words are still resounding –
Harken! jumbled noises spread
From the temple-gate's surrounding:
Thetis' famous son lies dead!
Eris shakes her snakes in daring,
All the gods they flee thereon,
And the Thund'rer's clouds are bearing
Darkly down on Ilion.

*Helen Kurz Roberts*

## DER RING DES POLYKRATES

Er stand auf seines Daches Zinnen,
Er schaute mit vergnügten Sinnen
Auf das beherrschte Samos hin.
„Dies alles ist mir untertänig",
Begann er zu Ägyptens König,
„Gestehe, daß ich glücklich bin!"

„Du hast der Götter Gunst erfahren!
Die vormals deinesgleichen waren,
Sie zwingt jetzt deines Zepters Macht;
Doch einer lebt noch, sie zu rächen:
Dich kann mein Mund nicht glücklich sprechen,
So lang des Feindes Auge wacht."

Und eh der König noch geendet,
Da stellt sich, von Milet gesendet,
Ein Bote dem Tyrannen dar:
„Laß, Herr, des Opfers Düfte steigen,
Und mit des Lorbeers muntern Zweigen
Bekränze dir dein festlich Haar.

Getroffen sank dein Feind vom Speere;
Mich sendet mit der frohen Märe
Dein treuer Feldherr Polydor –"
Und nimmt aus einem schwarzen Becken,
Noch blutig, zu der beiden Schrecken,
Ein wohlbekanntes Haupt hervor.

Der König tritt zurück mit Grauen:
„Doch warn ich dich, dem Glück zu trauen!"
Versetzt er mit besorgtem Blick.
„Bedenk, auf ungetreuen Wellen –
Wie leicht kann sie der Sturm zerschellen –
Schwimmt deiner Flotte zweifelnd Glück."

## THE RING OF POLYCRATES

Upon the palace-roof at leisure,
He stood and gazed with open pleasure
On Samos that he ruled of late.
"Behold this isle I am possessing,"
He said it, Egypt's king addressing,
"Admit that I am fortunate!"

"The gods have willed thy elevation!
And those who were of equal station,
They bow before thy sceptre's might.
Yet one avenger might yet shame thee,
And happy I cannot proclaim thee,
Thy foe is watching, day and night!"

Yet ere the king had finished speaking
An envoy from Milete came seeking
The tyrant's ear and spoke: "Have care,
And sacrifice and prayer render,
And laurel-branches, green and tender,
Entwine into thy festive hair!

"For Polydore, thy army leading,
With welcome tidings sent me speeding,
Thy foe, struck down by spears, is dead!"
And showing to the horror-shaken
What from a basin he had taken,
Lifts up a well-known, gory head.

The king at this steps back in horror.
Concerned he warns: "Avoid the error
Of trusting luck, for luck will cheat!
On treach'rous waves – thou shouldst be noting –
And tossed by tempests, there are floating
The dubious fortunes of thy fleet!"

Und eh er noch das Wort gesprochen,
Hat ihn der Jubel unterbrochen,
Der von der Reede jauchzend schallt:
Mit fremden Schätzen reich beladen,
Kehrt zu den heimischen Gestaden
Der Schiffe mastenreicher Wald.

Der königliche Gast erstaunet:
„Dein Glück ist heute gut gelaunet,
Doch fürchte seinen Unbestand.
Der Kreter waffenkund'ge Scharen
Bedräuen dich mit Kriegsgefahren;
Schon nahe sind sie diesem Strand."

Und eh ihm noch das Wort entfallen,
Da sieht mans von den Schiffen wallen,
Und tausend Stimmen rufen: „Sieg!
Von Feindesnot sind wir befreiet,
Die Kreter hat der Sturm zerstreuet,
Vorbei, geendet ist der Krieg!"

Das hört der Gastfreund mit Entsetzen:
„Fürwahr, ich muß dich glücklich schätzen,
Doch", spricht er, „zittr' ich für dein Heil;
Mir grauet vor der Götter Neide:
Des Lebens ungemischte Freude
Ward keinem Irdischen zuteil.

‚Auch mir ist alles wohl geraten;
Bei allen meinen Herrschertaten
Begleitet mich des Himmels Huld;
Doch hatt ich einen teuren Erben,
Den nahm mir Gott; ich sah ihn sterben,
Dem Glück bezahlt ich meine Schuld.

Drum, willst du dich·vor Leid bewahren,
So flehe zu den Unsichtbaren,
Daß sie zum Glück den Schmerz verleihn.

But barely was the sentence ended,
When shouts, of joy and triumph blended,
Rang out from every wharf and dike.
With foreign treasures richly laden,
Return unto their homeland-haven
The ships, high-masted, forest-like.

The royal guest is much astounded:
"Thy luck today appears unbounded,
Yet ever fear its fickleness!
The Cretan host, a martial nation,
They threaten war and tribulation;
Already towards this shore they press."

The final word he could not utter,
For from the ships arose a flutter
And thousands shouted: "Victory!
No more we fear. The foe is shattered!
The Cretan ships the storm has scattered,
And past are war and misery!"

The guest he hears it horrified.
"Thy luck, it cannot be denied,
Yet for thy safety I despair.
The jealous gods are not placated,
A life of bliss unmitigated,
Was never yet a mortal's share.

"I too achieved what I desired,
The sov'reign deeds that I inspired,
With heavenly approval met;
But him, the son and heir I cherished,
Him coveted the gods, he perished,
To fortune I have paid my debt.

"In order to avert disasters,
Thou shouldst implore thy unseen masters,
And woe, admixed with joy, demand.

Noch keinen sah ich fröhlich enden,
Auf den mit immer vollen Händen
Die Götter ihre Gaben streun.

Und wenns die Götter nicht gewähren,
So acht auf eines Freundes Lehren
Und rufe selbst das Unglück her;
Und was von allen deinen Schätzen
Dein Herz am höchsten mag ergetzen,
Das nimm und wirfs in dieses Meer!"

Und jener spricht, von Furcht beweget:
,,Von allem, was die Insel heget,
Ist dieser Ring mein höchstes Gut.
Ihn will ich den Erinnen weihen,
Ob sie mein Glück mir dann verzeihen –"
Und wirft das Kleinod in die Flut.

Und bei des nächsten Morgens Lichte,
Da tritt mit fröhlichem Gesichte
Ein Fischer vor den Fürsten hin:
,,Herr, diesen Fisch hab ich gefangen,
Wie keiner noch ins Netz gegangen;
Dir zum Geschenke bring ich ihn."

Und als der Koch den Fisch zerteilet,
Kommt er bestürzt herbeigeeilet
Und ruft mit hocherstauntem Blick:
,,Sieh, Herr, den Ring, den du getragen,
Ihn fand ich in des Fisches Magen;
O, ohne Grenzen ist dein Glück!"

Hier wendet sich der Gast mit Grausen:
,,So kann ich hier nicht ferner hausen,
Mein Freund kannst du nicht weiter sein.
Die Götter wollen dein Verderben –
Fort eil ich, nicht mit dir zu sterben."
Und sprachs und schiffte schnell sich ein.

His life in peace has never ended,
The one, on whom the gods expended
Their gifts with ever open hand.

"And if the gods ignore thy pleading,
My counsel, as a friend, be heeding
And court yourself adversity.
And what among thy splendid treasure
Delights thy heart in highest measure,
That take and throw into the sea!"

The other spoke, by fear inspired:
"This ring is what I most admired
Of all the goods these isles contain.
To Ye, Erínyés, I vow it,
My luck perchance, Ye will allow it,"
And throws the gem into the main.

And in the morn's irradiation,
His face aglow with jubilation,
A fisher to the tyrant came:
"My lord, this fish that I have netted,
So heavy that the cords were fretted,
As gift to thee I bring the same."

And when it was eviscerated,
The cook came running, agitated,
And cried, his eyes with wonder round:
"I found this ring, thou hadst been wearing,
Inside the fish I was preparing.
Thy luck, my lord, it knows no bound!"

The guest, he turned, his dread now stronger:
"I cannot stay here any longer,
Thy friendship is of no avail.
The gods decreed thou shouldst be dying.
To save myself I must be flying!"
He spoke, then ordered: "Hoist the sail!"

*Helen Kurz Roberts*

## DER TAUCHER

„Wer wagt es, Rittersmann oder Knapp,
Zu tauchen in diesen Schlund?
Einen goldnen Becher werf ich hinab,
Verschlungen schon hat ihn der schwarze Mund.
Wer mir den Becher kann wiederzeigen,
Er mag ihn behalten; er ist sein eigen."

Der König spricht es und wirft von der Höh'
Der Klippe, die schroff und steil
Hinaushängt in die unendliche See,
Den Becher in der Charybde Geheul.
„Wer ist der Beherzte, ich frage wieder,
Zu tauchen in diese Tiefe nieder?"

Und die Ritter, die Knappen um ihn her
Vernehmen's und schweigen still,
Sehen hinab in das wilde Meer,
Und keiner den Becher gewinnen will.
Und der König zum drittenmal wieder fraget:
„Ist keiner, der sich hinunterwaget?"

Doch alles noch stumm bleibt wie zuvor.
Und ein Edelknecht, sanft und keck,
Tritt aus der Knappen zagendem Chor,
Und den Gürtel wirft er, den Mantel weg,
Und alle die Männer umher und Frauen
Auf den herrlichen Jüngling verwundert schauen.

Und wie er tritt an des Felsen Hang
Und blickt in den Schlund hinab:
Die Wasser, die sie hinunterschlang,
Die Charybde jetzt brüllend wiedergab,
Und wie mit des fernen Donners Getose
Entstürzen sie schäumend dem finstern Schoße.

THE DIVER

"Who ventures, squire or fearless knight,
"To plunge down after this cup? –
"This precious goblet, with gold bedight –
"See how the whirlpool has swallowed it up!
"Whoever, among my train, retrieve it,
"Shall from my own hand, to keep, receive it."

The king had spoken, and hurled had he,
From the scarp so high and steep
That leaned out over the measureless sea,
The cup far into the roiling deep.
"Which daring heart my challenge misses?
"Again ask I, who will plumb the abysses?"

And the knights and the squires gave ear once again,
They listened, quiet and meek,
And looked down over the raging main,
Nor one made bold the cup to seek;
And the king, their eyes once more outstaring:
"Is there none among you with heart so daring?"

None stirred but for one lad, so strong,
So handsome, he made hearts melt,
Who came from out the reluctant throng
And doffed his cloak, ungirded his belt,
While the ladies and knights stood uneasy and waited
And watched the hero, their breath all bated.

Then forth to the rim of the cliff he stepped
And into the whirl he peered,
Where Charybdis, having stormed and leapt,
Spewed back the flood as she roared and reared,
And the billows, with sound of distant thunder,
Fought lest again she sucked them under.

Und es wallet und siedet und brauset und zischt,
Wie wenn Wasser mit Feuer sich mengt,
Bis zum Himmel spritzet der dampfende Gischt,
Und Flut auf Flut sich ohn Ende drängt,
Und will sich nimmer erschöpfen und leeren,
Als wollte das Meer noch ein Meer gebären.

Doch endlich, da legt sich die wilde Gewalt,
Und schwarz aus dem weißen Schaum
Klafft hinunter ein gähnender Spalt,
Grundlos, als gings in den Höllenraum,
Und reißend sieht man die brandenden Wogen
Hinab in den strudelnden Trichter gezogen.

Jetzt schnell, eh die Brandung wiederkehrt,
Der Jüngling sich Gott befiehlt,
Und – ein Schrei des Entsetzens wird rings gehört,
Und schon hat ihn der Wirbel hinweggespült,
Und geheimnisvoll über dem kühnen Schwimmer
Schließt sich der Rachen; er zeigt sich nimmer.

Und stille wirds über dem Wasserschlund,
In der Tiefe nur brauset es hohl;
Und bebend hört man von Mund zu Mund:
,,Hochherziger Jüngling, fahre wohl!"
Und hohler und hohler hört mans heulen,
Und es harrt noch mit bangem, mit schrecklichem Weilen.

Und wärfst du die Krone selber hinein
Und sprächst: Wer mir bringet die Kron,
Er soll sie tragen und König sein ! –
Mich gelüstete nicht nach dem teuren Lohn.
Was die heulende Tiefe da unten verhehle,
Das erzählt keine lebende, glückliche Seele !

They froth and they foam, they boil and they seethe,
As when water and fire meet,
The clouds and the heavens in spray were wreathed,
The waves trod on each other's feet,
No pause, no end to the ceaseless motion,
As ocean seemed to give birth to ocean.

At last a break in the turmoil fierce
And, black in the foaming white spume,
A yawning cleft the waters did pierce,
Unfathomed it was, like the depths of doom.
The court and the king watched the billows surging,
As slowly they followed the whirlpool's urging.

Quick now, before the surf could renew,
The youth to his God did pray.
A moan of horror went up from the crew
As he leapt and was lost in the whirling spray.
The waters closed o'er the daring swimmer.
The courtiers strained, but caught not a glimmer.

Then the maelstrom loosened its furious grip
But for rumblings and mutterings fell.
A whisper travelled from lip to lip:
"Stout-hearted youth, O fare thee well!"
Hollower now the whirlpool's howling
Still lingered with anxious and awesome growling.

And wert thou to hurl down the king's own crown
And spaketh: Whoe'er it retrieve,
He then shall wear it in ermine gown –
Not even such prize would I receive;
For of those deep secrets, grim and gory,
No living soul shall tell the story.

Wohl manches Fahrzeug, vom Strudel gefaßt,
Schoß gäh in die Tiefe hinab;
Doch zerschmettert nur rangen sich Kiel und Mast
Hervor aus dem alles verschlingenden Grab. –
Und heller und heller, wie Sturmes Sausen,
Hört mans näher und immer näher brausen.

Und es wallet und siedet und brauset und zischt,
Wie wenn Wasser mit Feuer sich mengt,
Bis zum Himmel spritzet der dampfende Gischt,
Und Well' auf Well' sich ohn' Ende drängt,
Und wie mit des fernen Donners Getose
Entstürzt es brüllend dem finstern Schoße.

Und sieh! aus dem finster flutenden Schoß
Da hebet sichs schwanenweiß,
Und ein Arm und ein glänzender Nacken wird bloß,
Und es rudert mit Kraft und mit emsigem Fleiß,
Und er ists, und hoch in seiner Linken
Schwingt er den Becher mit freudigem Winken.

Und atmete lang und atmete tief
Und begrüßte das himmlische Licht.
Mit Frohlocken es einer dem andern rief:
„Er lebt! Er ist da! Es behielt ihn nicht!
Aus dem Grab, aus der strudelnden Wasserhöhle
Hat der Brave gerettet die lebende Seele."

Und er kommt, es umringt ihn die jubelnde Schar,
Zu des Königs Füßen er sinkt.
Den Becher reicht er ihm kniend dar,
Und der König der lieblichen Tochter winkt,
Die füllt ihn mit funkelndem Wein bis zum Rande,
Und der Jüngling sich also zum König wandte:

Full many a vessel, caught in the whirl,
Plunged foully into the deep,
Which only keel and mast would hurl
Back upward again in shattered heap.
Onward and onward, like tempests roaring,
The wreckage-strewn waters come landward pouring.

They froth and they foam, they boil and they seethe,
As when water and fire meet.
The clouds and the heavens with spray they wreathe,
The waves tread on each other's feet,
And the billows, with sound of distant thunder,
Fight lest the whirlpool suck them under.

Behold! In the deep and somber green
A swanlike gleaming gain –
An arm and a heaving shoulder are seen,
They part the waters with might and main,
One hand the chalice gaily waving
For which the youth his fate was braving.

He breathèd deep and he breathèd long
And greeted the light of day;
And jubilant shouted the courtly throng:
"He lives! He has won over surf and spray!
From a watery grave he returns to the living,
Now let us bow in humble thanksgiving!"

Closer he draws and bends his knee,
As the courtiers wave and sing,
And proffers the cup for all to see –
To his winsome daughter beckons the king;
With sparkling wine she fills the chalice,
While the youth to his sovereign speaks without malice:

„Lang lebe der König! Es freue sich,
Wer da atmet im rosigten Licht!
Da unten aber ists fürchterlich,
Und der Mensch versuche die Götter nicht
Und begehre nimmer und nimmer zu schauen,
Was sie gnädig bedecken mit Nacht und Grauen.


Es riß mich hinunter blitzesschnell –
Da stürzt' mir aus felsigem Schacht
Wildflutend entgegen ein reißender Quell:
Mich packte des Doppelstroms wütende Macht,
Und wie einen Kreisel mit schwindelndem Drehen
Trieb michs um, ich konnte nicht widerstehen.


Da zeigte mir Gott, zu dem ich rief
In der höchsten schrecklichen Not,
Aus der Tiefe ragend ein Felsenriff,
Das erfaßt' ich behend und entrann dem Tod –
Und da hing auch der Becher an spitzen Korallen,
Sonst wär er ins Bodenlose gefallen.


Denn unter mir lags noch, bergetief,
In purpurner Finsternis da,
Und obs hier dem Ohre gleich ewig schlief,
Das Auge mit Schaudern hinuntersah,
Wies von Salamandern und Molchen und Drachen
Sich regt' in dem furchtbaren Höllenrachen.


Schwarz wimmelten da, in grausem Gemisch,
Zu scheußlichen Klumpen geballt,
Der stachligte Roche, der Klippenfisch,
Des Hammers greuliche Ungestalt,
Und dräuend wies mir die grimmigen Zähne
Der entsetzliche Hai, des Meeres Hyäne.

"Long live the king! Let all take cheer
Who in rosy light draw breath,
For horrible are the depths down there,
Nor let man challenge the gods and death,
Nor ever rue his merciful blindness
To horrors they hide in their wisdom and kindness.

"Downward and downward I plunged in a flash,
When out of a rocky chasm
A furious torrent me struck like a lash —
I was seized in the twin current's raging spasm,
And spun about, all turning and twisting,
A piece of jetsam, unresisting.

"I called out to God in my need and my grief,
Implored him to grant me aid,
When, rearing out of the depths, a reef
I seized, my certain death to evade,
And there the cup, on the coral grounded,
Which else would fain the depths have sounded.

"For under me the mountainous deep
In purple darkness lay,
And though to the ears there was nought but sleep,
The·flinching eye below could survey
A world of salamander and dragon
And in the deepest abyss, the Kraken.

"In black knots, fearsome and menacing,
Was seen the ugly swarm,
The vicious ray with his poisonous sting,
The hammerhead with his gruesome form,
And the scavenger of the sea's arena,
The shark, that underwater hyena.

Und da hing ich und wars mir mit Grausen bewußt,
Von der menschlichen Hilfe so weit,
Unter Larven die einzige fühlende Brust,
Allein in der gräßlichen Einsamkeit,
Tief unter dem Schall der menschlichen Rede
Bei den Ungeheuern der traurigen Öde.

Und schaudernd dacht' ich's, da kroch's heran,
Regte hundert Gelenke zugleich,
Will schnappen nach mir – in des Schreckens Wahn
Laß ich los der Koralle umklammerten Zweig;
Gleich faßt mich der Strudel mit rasendem Toben!
Doch es war mir zum Heil, er riß mich nach oben."

Der König darob sich verwundert schier
Und spricht: „Der Becher ist dein,
Und diesen Ring noch bestimm ich dir,
Geschmückt mit dem köstlichsten Edelgestein,
Versuchst du's noch einmal und bringst mir Kunde,
Was du sahst auf des Meeres tiefunterstem Grunde."

Das hörte die Tochter mit weichem Gefühl,
Und mit schmeichelndem Munde sie fleht:
„Laßt, Vater, genug sein das grausame Spiel!
Er hat Euch bestanden, was keiner besteht,
Und könnt Ihr des Herzens Gelüsten nicht zähmen,
So mögen die Ritter den Knappen beschämen."

Drauf der König greift nach dem Becher schnell,
In den Strudel ihn schleudert hinein:
„Und schaffst du den Becher mir wieder zur Stell',
So sollst du der trefflichste Ritter mir sein
Und sollst die als Ehgemahl heut' noch umarmen,
Die jetzt für dich bittet mit zartem Erbarmen."

"I clung there, fearfully oppressed,
No human aid in sight,
Among monsters the only sentient breast,
Alone in the dismal watery night,
Far beyond reach of friendly graces,
With nought but fiends in the desolate spaces.

"And hundred writhing, tentacled maws
Would take me in slimy embrace,
And hundred snapping, tooth-studded jaws
I fought, but needs must give way to their chase,
Let go of the coral, and upward was carried
In the arms of the whirlpool, else had I been buried."

Then gazed at the youth with marvel the king.
"The chalice is thine," quoth he;
And here is a prize to boot, this ring,
With jewels beset, I shall give to thee,
If thou venturest again and bringest back tiding
Of the nethermost creatures down there abiding."

The princess listed, her heart would fain
In her breast turn over; she pled:
"O Sire, desist from this cruel game,
Once has he returned from the realm of the dead,
If challenge thou must, him, prithee, send never,
Let one of thy knights the deed endeavor."

But swift for the cup the king did reach
And hurled it down below:
"The chalice again bring back to this beach,
And knighthood shall I on thee bestow —
This day shall see thee to altar leading
Her, here so fervently for thee pleading."

Da ergreift's ihm die Seele mit Himmelsgewalt,
Und es blitzt aus den Augen ihm kühn,
Und er siehet erröten die schöne Gestalt
Und sieht sie erbleichen und sinken hin –
Da treibts ihn, den köstlichen Preis zu erwerben,
Und stürzt sich hinunter auf Leben und Sterben.

Wohl hört man die Brandung, wohl kehrt sie zurück,
Sie verkündigt der donnernde Schall –
Da bückt sich's hinunter mit liebendem Blick:
Es kommen, es kommen die Wasser all,
Sie rauschen herauf, sie rauschen nieder,
Den Jüngling bringt keines wieder.

The youth to the depths of his soul was moved,
His eyes took courage soon;
He knew that each the other loved
As he saw the fair princess blush and swoon;
And he plunged down again, overpowered by desire,
Though it cost him his life, the prize to acquire.

The surf and the tide, they came and went,
Against the cliff they hurled;
Distraught from the brink the princess bent –
The waters washed and the waters swirled,
The waves grew higher, the waves grew fewer –
None returned the youthful wooer.

*Heinz Norden*

## DER KAMPF MIT DEM DRACHEN

Was rennt das Volk, was wälzt sich dort
Die langen Gassen brausend fort?
Stürzt Rhodus unter Feuers Flammen?
Es rottet sich im Sturm zusammen,
Und einen Ritter, hoch zu Roß,
Gewahr' ich aus dem Menschentroß;
Und hinter ihm, welch Abenteuer!
Bringt man geschleppt ein Ungeheuer;
Ein Drache scheint es von Gestalt
Mit weitem Krokodilesrachen,
Und alles blickt verwundert bald
Den Ritter an und bald den Drachen.

Und tausend Stimmen werden laut:
,,Das ist der Lindwurm, kommt und schaut,
Der Hirt und Herden uns verschlungen!
Das ist der Held, der ihn bezwungen!
Viel andre zogen vor ihm aus,
Zu wagen den gewalt'gen Strauß,
Doch keinen sah man wiederkehren;
Den kühnen Ritter soll man ehren!"
Und nach dem Kloster geht der Zug,
Wo Sankt Johanns des Täufers Orden,
Die Ritter des Spitals, im Flug
zu Rate sind versammelt worden.

Und vor den edeln Meister tritt
Der Jüngling mit bescheidnem Schritt;
Nachdrängt das Volk, mit wilden Rufen,
Erfüllend des Geländers Stufen.
Und jener nimmt das Wort und spricht:
,,Ich hab erfüllt die Ritterpflicht.

## THE DRAGON SLAYER

Why all the tumult? Out of doors
Why do the streets resound with roars?
Did Rhodes in flames and fire crumble
To call forth this fierce noise and rumble?
Behold! A knight, on charger proud,
Ride high above the clamoring crowd,
And after him an awesome creature
Drawn slowly forward, dread of feature –
A dragon seems it, by the shape,
With lizard maw that once spewed fire,
While young and old in wonder gape
Now at the beast, now at the squire.

And thousand voices rise in pitch:
"Behold the fearful monster which
Our herds and herdsmen sore has anquished –
The hero now the brute has vanquished!
Many an one before him went,
Like him upon the venture bent,
Nor ever from the quest returnèd;
Our gratitude the knight hath earnèd!"
Toward the monastery on
Now slowly moves the great procession,
Where sit the good knights of St. John,
The Hospitalers, met in session.

Unto his peers with modest mien
The youthful champion goes in,
While follow after him the rabble,
The cloisters filling with their babble.
Then to his fellows speaks the youth:
"The knightly deed is done, in truth,

Der Drache, der das Land verödet,
Er liegt von meiner Hand getötet;
Frei ist dem Wanderer der Weg,
Der Hirte treibe ins Gefilde,
Froh walle auf dem Felsensteg
Der Pilger zu dem Gnadenbilde."

Doch strenge blickt der Fürst ihn an
Und spricht: ,,Du hast als Held getan;
Der Mut ist's, der den Ritter ehret,
Du hast den kühnen Geist bewähret.
Doch sprich! Was ist die erste Pflicht
Des Ritters, der für Christum ficht,
Sich schmücket mit des Kreuzes Zeichen?"
Und alle rings herum erbleichen.
Doch er, mit edlem Anstand, spricht,
Indem er sich errötend neiget:
,,Gehorsam ist die erste Pflicht,
Die ihn des Schmuckes würdig zeiget."

,,Und diese Pflicht, mein Sohn," versetzt
Der Meister, ,,hast du frech verletzt.
Den Kampf, den das Gesetz versaget,
Hast du mit frevlem Mut gewaget!" –
,,Herr, richte, wenn du alles weißt,"
Spricht jener mit gesetztem Geist,
,,Denn des Gesetzes Sinn und Willen
Vermeint' ich treulich zu erfüllen.
Nicht unbedachtsam zog ich hin,
Das Ungeheuer zu bekriegen;
Durch List und kluggewandten Sinn
Versucht ich's, in dem Kampf zu siegen.

Fünf unsers Ordens waren schon,
Die Zierden der Religion,

The dragon who the land has wasted
Now from my hand his death has tasted;
The roads are free of gryphong wrath,
The herdsman safe, his flock attending,
So too the pilgrim, rocky path
To wonder-working shrine ascending."

The grand master austerely frowns:
"The hero's laurel thy brow crowns;
"Valor becomes the true knight errant;
Thy spirit has been perseverant;
Yet speak, what duty cometh first
And foremost with a knight who durst
Defend his Church and Christ, the Savior –
What rule, above all, guides his behavior?"
While all about grow pale, polite
Yet flushing speaks the liege, unflurried:
"Obedience firmly binds the knight,
Alone makes him his knighthood merit."

"This bounden duty," speaks the lord,
"Hast brazenly, my son, ignored;
The contest we ordained forbidden
To meet thou wantonly hast ridden!"
"Judge, Master, when thou all hast heard,"
The knight replied with measured word,
"For I have heeded thy injunction
With faithful and austere compunction,
Nor negligently did I choose
To meet this monstrous amphisbaena;
By clever artifice and ruse
Sought I to win in the arena.

"Five brethren of our order did –
Five pillars of our pious creed –

Des kühnen Mutes Opfer worden;
Da wehrtest du den Kampf dem Orden.
Doch an dem Herzen nagten mir
Der Unmut und die Streitbegier,
Ja, selbst im Traum der stillen Nächte
Fand ich mich keuchend im Gefechte;
Und wenn der Morgen dämmernd kam
Und Kunde gab von neuen Plagen,
Da faßte mich ein wilder Gram,
Und ich beschloß, es frisch zu wagen.

Und zu mir selber sprach ich dann:
Was schmückt den Jüngling, ehrt den Mann?
Was leisteten die tapfern Helden,
Von denen uns die Lieder melden,
Die zu der Götter Glanz und Ruhm
Erhub das blinde Heidentum?
Sie reinigten von Ungeheuern
Die Welt in kühnen Abenteuern,
Begegneten im Kampf dem Leun
Und rangen mit dem Minotauren,
Die armen Opfer zu befrein,
Und ließen sich das Blut nicht dauren.

Ist nur der Sarazen es wert,
Daß ihn bekämpft des Christen Schwert?
Bekriegt er nur die falschen Götter?
Gesandt ist er der Welt zum Retter;
Von jeder Not und jedem Harm
Befreien muß sein starker Arm;
Doch seinen Mut muß Weisheit leiten,
Und List muß mit der Stärke streiten.
So sprach ich oft und zog allein,
Des Raubtiers Fährte zu erkunden;

Fall victim to the monster feral
When thou forbadest further peril.
Yet discontent gnawed at my heart,
Nor would I with my purpose part
The brute to challenge. Even dreaming,
I scarcely ceased my furious scheming,
And when dawn, rising in the sky,
Would bring more news of his rapacious
Predations, firmly then would I
Resolve upon the deed audacious.

"And to myself then did I speak:
'What doth the warrior's honour eke,
Enhance the fame of knighthood's glory,
Of which we hear in song and story?
They brought the wretched heathen, blind,
Into God's fold and humankind;
They cleansed the world of fiend and dragon
In bold adventure and fierce agon;
On savage lion they waged war,
In combat met the Minotaur,
Victims enslaved to feedom leading,
Nor rued the blood which they were shedding.

" 'Is worthy but the Saracen
To taste the steel of Christian men?
Are we to fight but the blasphemers?
Are we then not the world's redeemers?
Of every danger, every harm,
Must free the earth our strong right arm;
Yet wisdom must our pluck be guiding,
With cunning over strength presiding.'
Thus to myself did oft I speak
And trailed the beast, to search and hound it;

Da flößte mir der Geist es ein,
Froh rief ich aus: Ich hab's gefunden!

Und trat zu dir und sprach das Wort:
Mich zieht es nach der Heimat fort.
Du, Herr, willfahrtest meinen Bitten,
Und glücklich war das Meer durchschnitten.
Kaum stieg ich aus am heim'schen Strand,
Gleich ließ ich durch des Künstlers Hand,
Getreu den wohlbemerkten Zügen,
Ein Drachenbild zusammenfügen.
Auf kurzen Füßen wird die Last
Des langen Leibes aufgetürmet;
Ein schuppicht Panzerhemd umfaßt
Den Rücken, den es furchtbar schirmet.

Lang streckte sich der Hals hervor,
Und gräßlich, wie ein Höllentor,
Als schmappt' es gierig nach der Beute,
Eröffnet sich des Rachens Weite,
Und aus dem schwarzen Schlunde dräun
Der Zähne stachelichte Reihn;
Die Zunge gleicht des Schwertes Spitze,
Die kleinen Augen sprühen Blitze;
In eine Schlange endigt sich
Des Rückens ungeheure Länge,
Rollt um sich selber fürchterlich,
Daß es um Mann und Roß sich schlänge.

Und alles bild' ich nach genau
Und kleid' es in ein scheußlich Grau;
Halb Wurm erschien's, halb Molch und Drache,
Gezeuget in der gift'gen Lache.
Und als das Bild vollendet war,

The answer came which I did seek,
And glad I cried out: 'I have found it!'

"And came to thee, and spoke the word:
'Lord, now the summons I have heard!'
Thou gavest consent to my notion;
Swiftly I crossed the inland ocean
And scarce debarked on homeland's strand,
I ordered made by artful hand,
Faithful in every vicious feature,
A model of the dragon creature.
Four thick, squat legs must serve to brace
The huge trunk that above them towered,
A coat of mail, a carapace,
To guard the wheels the engine powered.

"A long neck rose above the shell,
And dreadful, like the gates of hell,
From which there can be no escaping,
A pair of jaws, wide open, gaping;
And in that maw of cachalot,
Sharp teeth in serried row on row;
A tongue, swordlike and pointed, frightening,
Small bloodshot eyes, aflash with lightning;
Back, hump and crest toward the tail
Into a serpent's coils diminish,
Meant with its vicious lash and flail
Both horse and rider swift to finish.

"All this I wrought in wood and clay
And tinted it a dismal gray –
Half worm, half dragon, foul and rotten,
As though in poison swamp begotten –
And when the image was ordained,

Erwähl' ich mir ein Doggenpaar,
Gewaltig, schnell, von flinken Läufen,
Gewohnt, den wilden Ur zu greifen.
Die hetz' ich auf den Lindwurm an,
Erhitze sie zu wildem Grimme,
Zu fassen ihn mit scharfem Zahn,
Und lenke sie mit meiner Stimme.

Und wo des Bauches weiches Vließ
Den scharfen Bissen Blöße ließ,
Da reiz' ich sie, den Wurm zu packen,
Die spitzen Zähne einzuhacken.
Ich selbst, bewaffnet mit Geschoß,
Besteige mein arabisch Roß,
Von adeliger Zucht entstammet;
Und als ich seinen Zorn entflammet,
Rasch auf den Drachen spreng' ich's los
Und stachl' es mit den scharfen Sporen,
Und werfe zielend mein Geschoß,
Als wollt ich die Gestalt durchbohren.

Ob auch das Roß sich grauend bäumt
Und knirscht und in den Zügeln schäumt
Und meine Doggen ängstlich stöhnen,
Nicht rast' ich, bis sie sich gewöhnen.
So üb' ich's aus mit Emsigkeit,
Bis dreimal sich der Mond erneut;
Und als sie jedes recht begriffen,
Führ' ich sie her auf schnellen Schiffen.
Der dritte Morgen ist es nun,
Daß mir's gelungen, hier zu landen;
Den Gliedern gönnt' ich kaum zu ruhn,
Bis ich das große Werk bestanden.

Two mastiffs fierce I picked and trained,
Huge hounds, swift, savage, keen in tracking,
The wild aurochs skilled in attacking.
Them let I loose on the uncouth
Device, until, with bloodlust blinded,
They knew to fight it fang and tooth,
My every slightest order minded.

"And where the underbelly white
Lay open to their vicious bite,
I taught them well to dart and scurry,
The monster with their teeth to worry.
Myself, full-armed, would then proceed
To mount upon my Arab steed,
Of noble lineage the scion,
With speed of light and heart of lion.
Though he would rear and shy and prance,
I sped him on with reins and rowels
And aimed and hurled my trusty lance
As though to pierce the engine's bowels.

"My mount would neigh and paw the loam,
His bitted muzzle flecked with foam,
My dogs would whine and yelp and cower,
Yet soon I had them in my power;
The pallid moon thrice waxed and waned
While horse, hounds and myself I trained,
And when we all knew every motion,
Again I crossed the inland ocean.
Three mornings but have passed, 'tis true,
Since on these shores once more I landed;
Scarce did I sleep, intent to do
The awesome task my soul commanded.

Denn heiß erregte mir das Herz
Des Landes frisch erneuter Schmerz:
Zerrissen fand man jüngst die Hirten,
Die nach dem Sumpfe sich verirrten.
Und ich beschließe rasch die Tat,
Nur von dem Herzen nehm' ich Rat.
Flugs unterricht' ich meine Knappen,
Besteige den versuchten Rappen,
Und von dem edeln Doggenpaar
Begleitet, auf geheimen Wegen,
Wo meiner Tat kein Zeuge war,
Reit' ich dem Feinde frisch entgegen.

Das Kirchlein kennst du, Herr, das hoch
Auf eines Felsenberges Joch,
Der weit die Insel überschauet,
Des Meisters kühner Geist erbauet.
Verächtlich scheint es, arm und klein,
Doch ein Mirakel schließt es ein,
Die Mutter mit dem Jesusknaben,
Den die drei Könige begaben.
Auf dreimal dreißig Stufen steigt
Der Pilgrim nach der steilen Höhe;
Doch hat er schwindelnd sie erreicht,
Erquickt ihn seines Heilands Nähe.

Tief in den Fels, auf dem es hängt,
Ist eine Grotte eingesprengt,
Vom Tau des nahen Moors befeuchtet,
Wohin des Himmels Strahl nicht leuchtet.
Hier hausete der Wurm und lag,
Den Raub erspähend, Nacht und Tag.
So hielt er, wie der Höllendrache,
Am Fuß des Gotteshauses Wache;

"For sore aggrieved was my heart
To share our land's old sting and smart —
But recently another shepherd
Torn limb from limb in the swamp's jeopard!
Then with myself I counsel took —
No more delay the deed would brook;
I ached to march in every sinew
And swiftly marshaled my retinue;
Ahorse now, ushered by my dogs,
Onward I rode, avoiding witness,
On secret paths, through fields and bogs,
Against the beast to test my fitness.

"Thou knowest, Lord, the chapel high
On rocky mount up in the sky,
By master builder wrought, Elysian —
Far o'er our island goes its vision —
Which, seeming poor and mean and old,
A wondrous miracle doth hold:
The Virgin with the Jesus Child,
Adored by the Magi mild.
On three times thirty steps of stone
Behold the penitents ascending,
And, once the dizzy height is won,
Their souls with their Redeemer blending.

"A cave runs deep into the perch
Whereon is built the tiny church;
Dew-moistened from the near morasses,
This grotto sunlight never passes;
From here, the dragon's murky lair,
He scanned the valleys, prey to snare,
And, standing watch below the chapel,
With hapless wights was bent to grapple,

Und kam der Pilgrim hergewallt
Und lenkte in die Unglücksstraße,
Hervorbrach aus dem Hinterhalt
Der Feind und trug ihn fort zum Fraße.

Den Felsen stieg ich jetzt hinan,
Eh' ich den schweren Strauß begann;
Hin kniet' ich vor dem Christuskinde
Und reinigte mein Herz von Sünde.
Drauf gürt' ich mir im Heiligtum
Den blanken Schmuck der Waffen um,
Bewehre mit dem Spieß die Rechte,
Und nieder steig' ich zum Gefechte.
Zurücke bleibt der Knappen Troß;
Ich gebe scheidend die Befehle,
Und schwinge mich behend aufs Roß,
Und Gott empfehl' ich meine Seele.

Kaum seh' ich mich im ebnen Plan,
Flugs schlagen meine Doggen an,
Und bang beginnt das Roß zu keuchen
Und bäumet sich und will nicht weichen;
Denn nahe liegt, zum Knäul geballt,
Des Feindes scheußliche Gestalt
Und sonnet sich auf warmem Grunde.
Auf jagen ihn die flinken Hunde;
Doch wenden sie sich pfeilgeschwind,
Als es den Rachen gähnend teilet
Und von sich haucht den gift'gen Wind
Und winselnd wie der Schakal heulet.

Doch schnell erfrisch' ich ihren Mut,
Sie fassen ihren Feind mit Wut,
Indem ich nach des Tieres Lende
Aus starker Faust den Speer versende;

Whom, while upon their pilgrimage
Ascending to this airy bower,
He would assault in bloody rage,
Then in his cavern to devour.

"Ere I essayed the dreaded fray,
I climbed the mountain, there to pray
Before the Christ Child and the Virgin,
My heart of sin and frailty purging;
There, in that holy place, I donned
The naked arms that were my bond,
With javelin my right defended,
And to the battleground descended.
Made disposition, bade Godspeed
To them who faithful me attended,
Then swiftly mounted my strong steed,
My soul to God above commended.

"Scarce had I reached the valley's plain
When my two hounds gave tongue with main
And all at once my charger snorted,
For there, in noisome coils contorted,
The ghastly dragon lay, near by,
Who made both hounds and charger shy,
In sloth his ugly body sunning.
My dogs bethought them of their cunning,
Dodged in and out, defying death,
The snapping jaws to tease and tackle,
While the fierce brute, his poison breath
Exhaling, bellowed like a jackal.

"I cheered my hounds, as to and fro
They savagely attacked the foe,
The while I sought to speed his maiming,
My sharp lance at his withers aiming,

Doch machtlos, wie ein dünner Stab,
Prallt er vom Schuppenpanzer ab,
Und eh' ich meinen Wurf erneuet,
Da bäumet sich mein Roß und scheuet
An seinem Basiliskenblick
Und seines Atems gift'gem Wehen,
Und mit Entsetzen springt's zurück,
Und jetzo war's um mich geschehen.

Da schwing' ich mich behend vom Roß,
Schnell ist des Schwertes Schneide bloß;
Doch alle Streiche sind verloren,
Den Felsenharnisch zu durchbohren.
Und wütend mit des Schweifes Kraft
Hat es zur Erde mich gerafft;
Schon seh' ich seinen Rachen gähnen,
Es haut nach mir mit grimmen Zähnen
Als meine Hunde, wutentbrannt,
An seinen Bauch mit grimm'gen Bissen
Sich warfen, daß es heulend stand,
Von ungeheurem Schmerz zerissen.

Und, eh' es ihren Bissen sich
Entwindet, rasch erheb' ich mich,
Erspähe mir des Feindes Blöße
Und stoße tief ihm ins Gekröse,
Nachbohrend bis ans Heft den Stahl.
Schwarzquellend springt des Blutes Strahl,
Hin sinkt es und begräbt im Falle
Mich mit des Leibes Riesenballe,
Daß schnell die Sinne mir vergehn.
Und als ich neugestärkt erwache,
Seh' ich die Knappen um mich stehn,
Und tot im Blute liegt der Drache.''

Which, hurled with power, woe betide!
Bounced harmless from his scaly hide,
And ere I could again send flying
The spear, up reared my Arab, shying
Before this stare of basilisk,
This fetid breath's miasmic power,
Recoiling from death's fearful risk;
And now, I thought, had struck my hour.

"Then swiftly I dismounted, and
The sword's bare steel was in my hand;
Yet though I smote him, side and middle,
That scaly hide I could not riddle.
In turn, to his tail's furious lash
I fell and foundered with a crash;
Before his gaping jaws I quavered,
When my twain hounds, their muzzles slavered,
Attacked his underbelly, bared,
With vicious bites themselves disported;
And, roaring, up the dragon reared,
In mortal agony contorted.

"Before his bulk from jaws of hound
The brute could rescue, off the ground
I rose and, seeing dazed the lizard,
My sword drove deep into his gizzard
Unto the haft, twisted it good,
And black welled forth the creature's blood.
Then down he drooped and sank, and, falling,
He all but crushed me, sent me sprawling.
I struggled briefly, nought more knew;
When, later, I awoke, free-hearted,
About me stood my faithful crew –
There lay the beast, its life departed."

Des Beifalls lang gehemmte Lust
Befreit jetzt aller Hörer Brust,
So wie der Ritter dies gesprochen;
Und zehnfach am Gewölb gebrochen,
Wälzt der vermischten Stimmen Schall
Sich brausend fort im Widerhall.
Laut fordern selbst des Ordens Söhne,
Daß man die Heldenstirne kröne,
Und dankbar im Triumphgepräng
Will ihn das Volk dem Volke zeigen;
Da faltet seine Stirne streng
Der Meister und gebietet Schweigen.

Und spricht: ,,Den Drachen, der dies Land
Verheert, schlugst du mit tapfrer Hand;
Ein Gott bist du dem Volke worden –
Ein Feind kommst du zurück dem Orden,
Und einen schlimmern Wurm gebar
Dein Herz, als dieser Drache war.
Die Schlange, die das Herz vergiftet,
Die Zwietracht und Verderben stiftet,
Das ist der widerspenst'ge Geist,
Der gegen Zucht sich frech empöret,
Der Ordnung heilig Band zerreißt;
Denn der ist's, der die Welt zerstöret.''

Mut zeiget auch der Mameluck,
Gehorsam ist des Christen Schmuck;
Denn wo der Herr in seiner Größe
Gewandelt hat in Knechtesblöße,
Da stifteten, auf heil'gem Grund,
Die Väter dieses Ordens Bund,
Der Pflichten schwerste zu erfüllen,
Zu bändigen den eignen Willen.

To wild acclaim, so hardly pent,
The listeners now all give vent,
No sooner has the speaker finished;
And, by the echo undiminished,
Indeed, enhanced, the people's shout
Gains force and volume, rolling out.
"Let," cry the members of the order,
"The Abbot be the palm's awarder!"
And a procession forms somehow,
Not lacking much to be a riot.
The master sternly knits his brow,
Imperiously enjoining quiet.

"The dragon," he begins, "who lane
And field had ravaged hast thou slain.
The plaudits of the crowd thou earnest,
Yet as a foe to us returnest,
A fiercer dragon in thy heart
Than which did by thy sword depart;
That serpent, at thy heart now stinging,
Us discord and disaster bringing,
Our order's order shattering rude –
It is the spirit of defiance:
Here as outside it does denude
The bonds of discipline's compliance.

The Mameluke too can fight and ride –
Obedience is the Christian's pride;
'Twas in those sacred places, yonder,
Where once our Lord and God did wander,
Our founders built this brotherhood
To serve the sick and to do good
And to achieve that goal still vaster:
Our own defiant wills to master.

Dich hat der eitle Ruhm bewegt,
Drum wende dich aus meinen Blicken!
Denn wer des Herren Joch nicht trägt,
Darf sich mit seinem Kreuz nicht schmücken."

Da bricht die Menge tobend aus,
Gewalt'ger Sturm bewegt das Haus,
Um Gnade flehen alle Brüder;
Doch schweigend blickt der Jüngling nieder,
Still legt er von sich das Gewand
Und küßt des Meisters strenge Hand
Und geht. Der folgt ihm mit dem Blicke,
Dann ruft er liebend ihn zurücke
Und spricht: ,,Umarme mich, mein Sohn!
Dir ist der härt're Kampf gelungen.
Nimm dieses Kreuz. Es ist der Lohn
Der Demut, die sich selbst bezwungen."

Vainglory did but thee provoke,
So get thee hence, out of my vision;
For who refuse to bear Christ's yoke
To wear his cross have no permission."

A mighty roar swells from the crowd
Like tempest from a thundercloud;
The brethren clamor, mercy seeking;
The youth cast down his eyes, unspeaking;
He swiftly doffs his habit and,
Kissing his master's austere hand,
Departs. With loving eyes the master
Him follows, now averts disaster:
"Return!" he cries. "Embrace me, son!
This cross thou dost deserve. Receive it!
For greater struggle hast thou won.
Humility thou hast achieved."

*Heinz Norden*

## DIE BÜRGSCHAFT

Zu Dionys, dem Tyrannen, schlich
Damon, den Dolch im Gewande;
Ihn schlugen die Häscher in Bande.
„Was wolltest du mit dem Dolche, sprich!"
Entgegnet ihm finster der Wüterich. –
„Die Stadt vom Tyrannen befreien!"
„Das sollst du am Kreuze bereuen."

„Ich bin", spricht jener, „zu sterben bereit
Und bitte nicht um mein Leben;
Doch willst du Gnade mir geben,
Ich flehe dich um drei Tage Zeit,
Bis ich die Schwester dem Gatten gefreit;
Ich lasse den Freund dir als Bürgen –
Ihn magst du, entrinn' ich, erwürgen."

Da lächelt der König mit arger List
Und spricht nach kurzem Bedenken:
„Drei Tage will ich dir schenken.
Doch wisse: wenn sie verstrichen, die Frist,
Eh du zurück mir gegeben bist,
So muß er statt deiner erblassen,
Doch dir ist die Strafe erlassen."

Und er kommt zum Freunde: „Der König gebeut,
Daß ich am Kreuz mit dem Leben
Bezahle das frevelnde Streben;
Doch will er mir gönnen drei Tage Zeit,
Bis ich die Schwester dem Gatten gefreit,
So bleib du dem König zum Pfande,
Bis ich komme, zu lösen die Bande."

## THE SURETY

To the tyrant vile, Dionysius, went
One Damon, his dagger secreted;
His purpose the watchers defeated.
"Confess, what for was this dagger meant?"
Enquired the despot, his fury pent.
"To free from the tyrant my land!"
"On the cross thou shalt rue thy demand."

"I do not," the latter answers, "pray
For a life I am ready to offer;
Should mercy sway thee, then proffer
A respite and grant me three days' delay,
The time to give my sister away;
My friend be my pledge, I leave him,
To be killed should I fail to retrieve him."

The king thereat, smiling with sly intent,
Exclaims after short hesitation:
"I grant thee three days' prolongation;
But should thy term of reprieve be spent
Ere thou hast returned for thy punishment,
Then he, in thy stead stands committed,
He suffers, but thou art acquitted."

And he comes to his friend: "On the cross I must pay
With my life for the crime I intended.
Yet the king who decreed it unbended
And, merciful, granted me three days' delay,
The time to give my sister away;
Stay thou with the king for assurance,
Till I come to release thee from durance."

Und schweigend umarmt ihn der treue Freund
Und liefert sich aus dem Tyrannen,
Der andere ziehet von dannen.
Und ehe das dritte Morgenrot scheint,
Hat er schnell mit dem Gatten die Schwester vereint,
Eilt heim mit sorgender Seele,
Damit er die Frist nicht verfehle.

Da gießt unendlicher Regen herab,
Von den Bergen stürzen die Quellen,
Und die Bäche, die Ströme schwellen.
Und er kommt ans Ufer mit wanderndem Stab,
Da reißet die Brücke der Strudel hinab,
Und donnernd sprengen die Wogen
Des Gewölbes krachenden Bogen.

Und trostlos irrt er an Ufers Rand:
Wie weit er auch spähet und blicket
Und die Stimme, die rufende, schicket –
Da stößet kein Nachen vom sichern Strand,
Der ihn setze an das gewünschte Land,
Kein Schiffer lenket die Fähre,
Und der wilde Strom wird zum Meere.

Da sinkt er ans Ufer und weint und fleht,
Die Hände zum Zeus erhoben:
„O hemme des Stromes Toben!
Es eilen die Stunden, im Mittag steht
Die Sonne, und wenn sie niedergeht
Und ich kann die Stadt nicht erreichen,
So muß der Freund mir erbleichen."

Doch wachsend erneut sich des Stromes Wut,
Und Welle auf Welle zerrinnet,
Und Stunde an Stunde entrinnet,

In his silence, the friend enclasps him, betakes
Himself to the king to surrender;
On his errand sets out the offender.
And ere yet the dawn of the third day breaks,
The newly married pair he forsakes,
Turns homeward, with anxious desire,
Lest the term of his respite expire.

But rain, unending, pours down all day,
Each mountain-spring, torrentlike, gushes,
In spate, the river rushes.
On reaching the shore he sees with dismay
The vortex tearing the bridge away,
And thundering waves are assaulting
The cracking arch of the vaulting.

Despairing, he wanders about on the strand;
Yet wherever he searches and gazes
And his questing voice upraises,
No boat that would leave the sheltering land
To ferry him over at his command,
No skipper to guide its motion,
And the river becomes an ocean.

He sinks down on the bank in fear and fret
And prays unto Zeus: "Oh, deliver
These shores from the rage of the river!
The hours are flying, the sun as yet
Is high at the noon, but should it set
Ere I reach the gate of the city,
My friend has to die; oh take pity!"

Yet with growing fury the river raves
And wave after wave is massing,
And hour after hour is passing.

Da treibt ihn die Angst, da faßt er sich Mut
Und wirft sich hinein in die brausende Flut
Und teilt mit gewaltigen Armen
Den Strom, und ein Gott hat Erbarmen.

Und gewinnt das Ufer und eilet fort
Und danket dem rettenden Gotte;
Da stürzet die raubende Rotte
Hervor aus des Waldes nächtlichem Ort,
Den Pfad ihm sperrend, und schnaubet Mord
Und hemmet des Wanderers Eile
Mit drohend geschwungener Keule.

„Was wollt ihr?" ruft er, für Schrecken bleich;
„Ich habe nichts als mein Leben,
Das muß ich dem Könige geben!"
Und entreißt die Keule dem nächsten gleich:
„Um des Freundes willen erbarmet euch!"
Und drei, mit gewaltigen Streichen,
Erlegt er, die andern entweichen.

Und die Sonne versendet glühenden Brand,
Und von der unendlichen Mühe
Ermattet, sinken die Kniee:
„O, hast du mich gnädig aus Räuberhand,
Aus dem Strom mich gerettet ans heilige Land,
Und soll hier verschmachtend verderben,
Und der Freund mir, der liebende, sterben!"

Und horch! da sprudelt es silberhell
Ganz nahe, wie rieselndes Rauschen,
Und stille hält er zu lauschen;
Und sieh, aus dem Felsen, geschwätzig, schnell,
Springt murmelnd hervor ein lebendiger Quell,
Und freudig bückt er sich nieder
Und erfrischet die brennenden Glieder.

Then, driven by fear, the danger he braves
And plunging into the onrushing waves
He cleaves in a powerful fashion
The floods, and a god shows compassion.

He reaches the shore and proceeds; yet first
Gives thanks to the godhead that aided;   •
But robbers, that plundered and raided,
From the forest's benighted shelter burst
And barring his way, for blood athirst,
Are checking the wanderer's paces,
Abrandishing menacing maces.

"What is it ye want?" he exclaims in fear,
"My life is my only possession,
And that is the king's for transgression!"
He snatches the club from the one who is near:
"Give way, for the sake of the friend I hold dear!"
And with powerful blows he batters
Just three; the remainder scatters.

And the sun beats down, a fiery brand,
And from all these efforts, unending,
His weary knees are bending.
"Hast thou graciously saved me from robber-hand,
From the river onto the sacred land
That, parched, I shall here have to perish,
Undoing the friend I most cherish?"

But hark! a murmur falls on his ear,
A purling and rippling, to listen
He stops and perceives a glisten;
And lo! a source from the rock-face near,
With lively babbling springs silvery clear,
And joyful he stoops to the pouring,
His burning limbs restoring.

Und die Sonne blickt durch der Zweige Grün
Und malt auf den glänzenden Matten
Der Bäume gigantische Schatten;
Und zwei Wanderer sieht er die Straße ziehn,
Will eilenden Laufes vorüberfliehn,
Da hört er die Worte sie sagen:
„Jetzt wird er ans Kreuz geschlagen."

Und die Angst beflügelt den eilenden Fuß,
Ihn jagen der Sorge Qualen;
Da schimmern in Abendrots Strahlen
Von ferne die Zinnen von Syrakus,
Und entgegen kommt ihm Philostratus,
Des Hauses redlicher Hüter,
Der erkennet entsetzt den Gebieter:

„Zurück! du rettest den Freund nicht mehr,
So rette das eigene Leben!
Den Tod erleidet er eben.
Von Stunde zu Stunde gewartet' er
Mit hoffender Seele der Wiederkehr,
Ihm konnte den mutigen Glauben
Der Hohn des Tyrannen nicht rauben."

„Und ist es zu spät, und kann ich ihm nicht
Ein Retter willkommen erscheinen,
So soll mich der Tod ihm vereinen.
Des rühme der blut'ge Tyrann sich nicht,
Daß der Freund dem Freunde gebrochen die Pflicht –
Er schlachte der Opfer zweie
Und glaube an Liebe und Treue."

Und die Sonne geht unter, da steht er am Tor
Und sieht das Kreuz schon erhöhet,
Das die Menge gaffend umstehet;

Through leafy branches the sunbeams cast
Upon the gleaming meadows
The trees' gigantic shadows;
Two wand'rers he sees on the road, and as fast
He draws abreast and is flying past,
He hears them say, ere they hail him:
"Anon to the cross they nail him."

And anguish lends wings to limbs out of use,
He is driven by fear, ever growing,
When he sees, in the sunset glowing,
The distant towers of Syracuse,
And he meets the honest Philostratus,
His steward, who true in disaster,
Exclaims at the sight of his master:

"Go back! his life is beyond thy concern,
For thy own thou shouldst be flying!
Just now, on the cross, he is dying.
From hour to hour he waited to learn,
With hope in his heart, of thy timely return,
And the tyrant's derisive predictions
Could not shake his courageous convictions."

'Too late though to save him from such an end,
I keep yet the troth I have plighted.
In death we shall be reunited.
The bloodthirsty tyrant shall never pretend
That a friend has broken his pledge to a friend.
He may slaughter me like the other.
Neither love nor faith he can smother!"

As the sun is setting he stands by the gate
The cross is already erected,
And a gaping crowd has collected;

An dem Seile schon zieht man den Freund empor,
Da zertrennt er gewaltig den dichten Chor:
„Mich, Henker!" ruft er, „erwürget!
Da bin ich, für den er gebürget!"

Und Erstaunen ergreifet das Volk umher,
In den Armen liegen sich beide
Und weinen für Schmerzen und Freude.
Da sieht man kein Auge tränenleer,
Und zum Könige bringt man die Wundermär';
Der fühlt ein menschliches Rühren,
Läßt schnell vor den Thron sie führen.

Und blicket sie lange verwundert an;
Drauf spricht er: „Es ist euch gelungen,
Ihr habt das Herz mir bezwungen,
Und die Treue, sie ist doch kein leerer Wahn –
So nehmet auch mich zum Genossen an.
Ich sei, gewährt mir die Bitte,
In eurem Bunde der dritte."

By a rope they are hauling up his mate
As he cleaves the masses, exclaiming: "Wait,
Executioner, kill me, reprieve him
Who stood surety for me, I relieve him!"

Astonishment grips the people that hear,
In each other's arms they are lying,
For joy and sorrow crying.
No eye can be seen without a tear,
The wonder tale reaches the tyrant's ear;
A human emotion comes o'er him
And he has them brought before him.

And looks at them long and cannot supress
His wonder. Then speaks: "Ye contrived it,
My unfeeling heart, ye revived it;
No empty illusion is faithfulness –
As a comrade accept me, pray acquiesce:
Let me be, by your compliance,
The third in your alliance!"

*Helen Kurz Roberts*

## DER HANDSCHUH

Vor seinem Löwengarten,
Das Kampfspiel zu erwarten,
Saß König Franz,
Und um ihn die Großen der Krone,
Und rings auf hohem Balkone
Die Damen in schönem Kranz.

Und wie er winkt mit dem Finger,
Auf tut sich der weite Zwinger,
Und hinein mit bedächtigem Schritt
Ein Löwe tritt
Und sieht sich stumm
Rings um
Mit langem Gähnen
Und schüttelt die Mähnen
Und streckt die Glieder
Und legt sich nieder.

Und der König winkt wieder,
Da öffnet sich behend
Ein zweites Tor,
Daraus rennt
Mit wildem Sprunge
Ein Tiger hervor.
Wie der den Löwen erschaut,
Brüllt er laut,
Schlägt mit dem Schweif
Einen furchtbaren Reif
Und recket die Zunge,
Und im Kreise scheu
Umgeht er den Leu

## THE GLOVE

Before his lion-court,
Awaiting bloody sport,
Sat Francis the King,
About him the nobles of station,
Above, in lovely curvation,
The ladies, in balcony-ring.

And as his finger is raised, inside
The great arena opens wide
And, striding forth with regal mien
A lion is seen.
Without a sound
He stares around
And yawns disdain,
And shakes his mane,
And stretches, shows a frown,
And then lies down.

And again at a sign from the king,
There opens in the ring
A second cage,
And from it in rage
And greedy for feast
Bounds a tiger-beast.
As he the lion espies,
He roars to the skies
And lashes his tail
Like the sweep of a flail,
His fangs he shows
And cautiously goes
In a circle that
Is safe from the lion-cat;

Grimmig schnurrend;
Drauf streckt er sich murrend
Zur Seite nieder.


Und der König winkt wieder,
Da speit das doppelt geöffnete Haus
Zwei Leoparden auf einmal aus.
Die stürzen mit mutiger Kampfbegier
Auf das Tigertier;
Das packt sie mit seinen grimmigen Tatzen,
Und der Leu mit Gebrüll
Richtet sich auf – da wirds still;
Und herum im Kreis,
Von Mordsucht heiß,
Lagern sich die greulichen Katzen.


Da fällt von des Altans Rand
Ein Handschuh von schöner Hand
Zwischen den Tiger und den Leun
Mitten hinein.


Und zu Ritter Delorges spottenderweis
Wendet sich Fräulein Kunigund:
,,Herr Ritter, ist eure Lieb so heiß,
Wie ihr mirs schwört zu jeder Stund,
Ei, so hebt mir den Handschuh auf!"


Und der Ritter, in schnellem Lauf,
Steigt hinab in den furchtbaren Zwinger
Mit festem Schritte,
Und aus der Ungeheuer Mitte
Nimmt er den Handschuh mit keckem Finger.

Then, angrily growling,
He crouches, still prowling,
At the side of the den.


And the king signs again;
The gates now open doubly wide,
Spew forth two leopards side by side,
Who pounce with lust for a battle-feast
Upon the tiger-beast;
But he takes hold with murderous claws,
And the lion, shaking his mane,
Roars loud, makes silence reign.
While round in a ring,
Fight-quivering,
Lie the cats, licking their jaws.


Just then, from the balcony's rail,
The glove of a fair hand and frail
Falls in the lion and tiger domain,
Twixt the twain.


And to Sir Delorges, in mockery gay,
Turns Lady Cunigonda, to say:
"Sir Knight, if your love be truly so warm,
As daily and every hour you've sworn,
Well, then fetch back my glove for me!"


And the knight unhesitantly
To the den of horror descends,
Firm steps he makes,
His impudent finger extends,
And the glove from the ring of beasts he takes.

Und mit Erstaunen und mit Grauen
Sehens die Ritter und Edelfrauen,
Und gelassen bringt er den Handschuh zurück.
Da schallt ihm sein Lob aus jedem Munde,
Aber mit zärtlichem Liebesblick –
Er verheißt ihm sein nahes Glück –
Empfängt ihn Fräulein Kunigunde.
Und er wirft ihr den Handschuh ins Gesicht:
„Den Dank, Dame, begehr' ich nicht!"
Und verläßt sie zur selben Stunde.

And with amazement and terror the sight
Is observed by each lady and knight,
As unperturbed he returns with the glove.
His praises then ring in the air,
And Cunigonda, the fair,
Now greets him with glances of tender love –
They promise him all her beauty's sweet flower –
And he just flings the glove in her face:
"Your thanks I do not desire, Your Grace!"
And leaves her in that selfsame hour.

*Harold Lenz*

## DAS LIED VON DER GLOCKE

Vivos voco. Mortuos plango. Fulgura frango

Fest gemauert in der Erden
Steht die Form, aus Lehm gebrannt.
Heute muß die Glocke werden!
Frisch, Gesellen, seid zur Hand!
    Von der Stirne heiß
    Rinnen muß der Schweiß,
Soll das Werk den Meister loben;
Doch der Segen kommt von oben.

Zum Werke, das wir ernst bereiten,
Geziemt sich wohl ein ernstes Wort;
Wenn gute Reden sie begleiten,
Dann fließt die Arbeit munter fort.
So laßt uns jetzt mit Fleiß betrachten,
Was durch die schwache Kraft entspringt;
Den schlechten Mann muß man verachten,
Der nie bedacht, was er vollbringt.
Das ists ja, was den Menschen zieret,
Und dazu ward ihm der Verstand,
Daß er im innern Herzen spüret,
Was er erschafft mit seiner Hand.

Nehmet Holz vom Fichtenstamme,
Doch recht trocken laßt es sein,
Daß die eingepreßte Flamme
Schlage zu dem Schwalch hinein!
    Kocht des Kupfers Brei,
    Schnell das Zinn herbei,
Daß die zähe Glockenspeise
Fließe nach der rechten Weise!

## SONG OF THE BELL

Vivos voco. Mortuos plango. Fulgura frango

Fastened deep in firmest earth,
Stands the mold of well-burnt clay.
Now we'll give the bell its birth;
Quick, my friends, no more delay!
  From the heated brow
  Sweat must freely flow,
If to your master praise be given:
But the blessing comes from Heaven.

To the work we now prepare
A serious thought is surely due;
And cheerfully the toil we'll share,
If cheerful words be mingled too.
Then let us still with care observe
What from our strength, yet weakness, springs;
For he respect can ne'er deserve
Who hands alone to labor brings.
'Tis only this which honors man:
His mind with heavenly fire was warmed,
That he with deepest thought might scan
The work which his own hand has formed.

  With splinters of the driest pine
  Now feed the fire below;
  Then the rising flame shall shine,
  And the melting ore shall flow.
    Boils the brass within,
    Quickly add the tin;
  That the thick metallic mass
  Rightly to the mold may pass.

Was in des Dammes tiefer Grube
Die Hand mit Feuers Hilfe baut,
Hoch auf des Turmes Glockenstube,
Da wird es von uns zeugen laut.
Noch dauern wirds in späten Tagen
Und rühren vieler Menschen Ohr
Und wird mit dem Betrübten klagen
Und stimmen zu der Andacht Chor.
Was unten tief dem Erdensohne
Das wechselnde Verhängnis bringt,
Das schlägt an die metallne Krone,
Die es erbaulich weiterklingt.

Weiße Blasen seh ich springen,
Wohl! die Massen sind im Fluß.
Laßts mit Aschensalz durchdringen,
Das befördert schnell den Guß.
Auch vom Schaume rein
Muß die Mischung sein,
Daß vom reinlichen Metalle
Rein und voll die Stimme schalle.

Denn mit der Freude Feierklange
Begrüßt sie das geliebte Kind
Auf seines Lebens erstem Gange,
Den es in Schlafes Arm beginnt.
Ihm ruhen noch im Zeitenschoße
Die schwarzen und die heitern Lose;
Der Mutterliebe zarte Sorgen
Bewachen seinen goldnen Morgen. —
Die Jahre fliehen pfeilgeschwind.
Vom Mädchen reißt sich stolz der Knabe,
Er stürmt ins Leben wild hinaus,
Durchmißt die Welt am Wanderstabe.

What with the aid of fire's dread power
We in the dark, deep pit now hide,
Shall, on some lofty, sacred tower,
Tell of our skill and form our pride.
And it shall last to days remote,
Shall thrill the ear of many a race;
Shall sound with sorrow's mournful note,
And call to pure devotion's grace.
Whatever to the sons of earth
Their changing destiny brings down,
To the deep solemn clang gives birth,
That rings from out this metal crown.

See, the boiling surface, whitening,
Shows the whole is mixing well;
Add the salts, the metal brightening,
Ere flows out the liquid bell.
Clear from foam or scum
Must the mixture come,
That with a rich metallic note
The sound aloft in air may float.

Now with joy and festive mirth
Salute that loved and lovely child,
Whose earliest moments on the earth
Are passed in sleep's dominion mild.
While on Time's lap he rests his head,
The fatal sisters spin their thread;
A mother's love, with softest rays,
Gilds o'er the morning of his days. –
But years with arrowy haste are fled.
His nursery bonds he proudly spurns;
He rushes to the world without;
After long wandering, home he turns,

Fremd kehrt er heim ins Vaterhaus,
Und herrlich, in der Jugend Prangen,
Wie ein Gebild aus Himmelshöhn,
Mit züchtigen, verschämten Wangen
Sieht er die Jungfrau vor sich stehn.
Da faßt ein namenloses Sehnen
Des Jünglings Herz, er irrt allein,
Aus seinen Augen brechen Tränen,
Er flieht der Brüder wilden Reihn.
Errötend folgt er ihren Spuren
Und ist von ihrem Gruß beglückt,
Das Schönste sucht er auf den Fluren,
Womit er seine Liebe schmückt.
O zarte Sehnsucht, süßes Hoffen,
Der ersten Liebe goldne Zeit!
Das Auge sieht den Himmel offen,
Es schwelgt das Herz in Seligkeit –
O daß sie ewig grünen bliebe,
Die schöne Zeit der jungen Liebe!

Wie sich schon die Pfeifen bräunen!
Dieses Stäbchen tauch ich ein:
Sehn wirs überglast erscheinen,
Wirds zum Gusse zeitig sein.
Jetzt, Gesellen, frisch!
Prüft mir das Gemisch,
Ob das Spröde mit dem Weichen
Sich vereint zum guten Zeichen.

Denn wo das Strenge mit dem Zarten,
Wo Starkes sich und Mildes paarten,
Da gibt es einen guten Klang.
Drum prüfe, wer sich ewig bindet,
Ob sich das Herz zum Herzen findet!
Der Wahn ist kurz, die Reu ist lang.
Lieblich in der Bräute Locken

Arrives a stranger and in doubt.
There, lovely in her beauty's youth,
  A form of heavenly mold he meets,
Of modest air and simple truth;
  The blushing maid he bashful greets.
A nameless feeling seizes strong
  On his young heart. He walks alone;
To his moist eyes emotions throng;
  His joy in ruder sports has flown.
He follows, blushing, where she goes;
  And should her smile but welcome him,
The fairest flower, the dewy rose,
  To deck her beauty seems too dim.
O tenderest passion! Sweetest hope!
  The golden hours of earliest love!
Heaven's self to him appears to ope;
  He feels a bliss this earth above.
Oh, that it could eternal last!
That youthful love were never past!

  See how brown the liquid turns!
  Now this rod I thrust within;
  If it's glazed before it burns,
  Then the casting may begin.
    Quick, my lads, and steady,
    If the mixture's ready!
  When the strong and weaker blend,
  Then we hope a happy end:

Whenever strength with softness joins,
When with the rough the mild combines,
Then all is union sweet and strong.
Consider, ye who join your hands,
If hearts are twined in mutual bands;
For passion's brief, repentance long.
How lovely in the maiden's hair

Spielt der jungfräuliche Kranz,
Wenn die hellen Kirchenglocken
Laden zu des Festes Glanz.
Ach! des Lebens schönste Feier
Endigt auch den Lebensmai,
Mit dem Gürtel, mit dem Schleier
Reißt der schöne Wahn entzwei.
Die Leidenschaft flieht,
Die Liebe muß bleiben,
Die Blume verblüht,
Die Frucht muß treiben.
Der Mann muß hinaus
Ins feindliche Leben,
Muß wirken und streben
Und pflanzen und schaffen,
Erlisten, erraffen,
Muß wetten und wagen,
Das Glück zu erjagen.
Da strömet herbei die unendliche Gabe,
Es füllt sich der Speicher mit köstlicher Habe,
Die Räume wachsen, es dehnt sich das Haus.

Und drinnen waltet
Die züchtige Hausfrau,
Die Mutter der Kinder,
Und herrschet weise
Im häuslichen Kreise,
Und lehret die Mädchen
Und wehret den Knaben
Und reget ohn Ende
Die fleißigen Hände
Und mehrt den Gewinn
Mit ordnendem Sinn,
Und füllet mit Schätzen die duftenden Laden
Und dreht um die schnurrende Spinde den Faden,
Und sammelt im reinlich geglätteten Schrein

The bridal garland plays!
And merry bells invite us there,
Where mingle festive lays.
Alas! that all life's brightest hours
Are ended with its earliest May!
That from those sacred nuptial bowers
The dear deceit should pass away!
Though passion may fly,
Yet love will endure;
The flower must die,
The fruit to insure.
The man must without,
Into struggling life;
With toiling and strife,
He must plan and contrive;
Must be prudent to thrive;
With boldness must dare,
Good fortune to share.
'Tis by means such as these, that abundance is poured
In a full, endless stream, to increase all his hoard,
While his house to a palace spreads out.

Within doors governs
The modest, careful wife,
The children's kind mother;
And wise is the rule
Of her household school.
She teaches the girls,
And she warns the boys;
She directs all the bands
Of diligent hands,
And increases their gain
By her orderly reign.
And she fills with her treasures her sweet-scented chests
From the toil of her spinning-wheel scarcely she rests;
And she gathers in order, so cleanly and bright,

Die schimmernde Wolle, den schneeigten Lein,
Und füget zum Guten den Glanz und den Schimmer,
Und ruhet nimmer.

Und der Vater mit frohem Blick
Von des Hauses weitschauendem Giebel
Überzählet sein blühend Glück,
Siehet der Pfosten ragende Bäume
Und der Scheunen gefüllte Räume
Und die Speicher, vom Segen gebogen,
Und des Kornes bewegte Wogen,
Rühmt sich mit stolzem Mund:
Fest, wie der Erde Grund,
Gegen des Unglücks Macht
Steht mir des Hauses Pracht! –
Doch mit des Geschickes Mächten
Ist kein ew'ger Bund zu flechten,
Und das Unglück schreitet schnell.

Wohl! nun kann der Guß beginnen,
Schön gezacket ist der Bruch.
Doch, bevor wirs lassen rinnen,
Betet einen frommen Spruch!
Stoßt den Zapfen aus!
Gott bewahr das Haus!
Rauchend in des Henkels Bogen
Schießts mit feuerbraunen Wogen.

Wohltätig ist des Feuers Macht,
Wenn sie der Mensch bezähmt, bewacht,
Und was er bildet, was er schafft,
Das dankt er dieser Himmelskraft;
Doch furchtbar wird die Himmelskraft,
Wenn sie der Fessel sich entrafft,
Einhertritt auf der eigenen Spur
Die freie Tochter der Natur.

The softest of wool, and the linen snow-white:
The useful and pleasant she mingles ever,
And is slothful never.

The father, cheerful, from the door,
His wide-extended homestead eyes;
Tells all his smiling fortunes o'er;
The future columns in his trees,
His barn's well furnished stock he sees,
His granaries e'en now o'erflowing,
While yet the waving corn is growing.
He boasts with swelling pride,
"Firm as the mountain's side
Against the shock of fate
Is now my happy state."
Who can discern futurity?
Who can insure prosperity?
Quick misfortune's arrow flies.

   Now we may begin to cast;
   All is right and well prepared:
   Yet, ere the anxious moment's past,
   A pious hope by all be shared.
      Strike the stopper clear!
      God preserve us here!
   Sparkling, to the rounded mold
   It rushes hot, like liquid gold.

How useful is the power of flame,
If human skill control and tame!
And much of all that man can boast,
Without this child of Heaven, were lost.
But frightful is her changing mien,
When, bursting from her bonds, she's seen
To quit the safe and quiet hearth,
And wander lawless o'er the earth.

Wehe, wenn sie losgelassen,
Wachsend ohne Widerstand
Durch die volkbelebten Gassen
Wälzt den ungeheuren Brand!
Denn die Elemente hassen
Das Gebild der Menschenhand.
Aus der Wolke
Quillt der Segen,
Strömt der Regen
Aus der Wolke, ohne Wahl,
Zuckt der Strahl!
Hört ihrs wimmern hoch vom Turm?
Das ist Sturm!
Rot wie Blut
Ist der Himmel,
Das ist nicht des Tages Glut!
Welch Getümmel
Straßen auf!
Dampf wallt auf!
Flackernd steigt die Feuersäule,
Durch der Straße lange Zeile
Wächst es fort mit Windeseile,
Kochend, wie aus Ofens Rachen,
Glühn die Lüfte, Balken krachen,
Pfosten stürzen, Fenster klirren,
Kinder jammern, Mütter irren,
Tiere wimmern
Unter Trümmern.
Alles rennet, rettet, flüchtet,
Taghell ist die Nacht gelichtet.
Durch der Hände lange Kette
Um die Wette
Fliegt der Eimer, hoch im Bogen
Spritzen Quellen, Wasserwogen.
Heulend kommt der Sturm geflogen,
Der die Flamme brausend sucht.

Woe to those whom then she meets!
Against her fury who can stand?
Along the thickly peopled streets
She madly hurls her fearful brand.
Then the elements, with joy,
Man's best handiwork destroy.
From the clouds
Falls amain
The blessed rain:
From the clouds alike
Lightnings strike.
Ringing loud the fearful knell
Sounds the bell.
Dark blood-red
Are all the skies;
But no dawning light is spread.
What wild cries
From the streets arise!
Smoke dims the eyes.
Flickering mounts the fiery glow
Along the street's extended row,
Fast as fiercest winds can blow.
Bright, as with a furnace flare,
And scorching, is the heated air;
Beams are falling, children crying,
Windows breaking, mothers flying,
Creatures moaning, crushed and dying, –
All is uproar, hurry, flight,
And light as day the dreadful night.
Along the eager living lane,
Though all in vain,
Speeds the bucket. The engine's power
Sends the artificial shower.
But see, the heavens still threatening lower!
The winds rush roaring to the flame.

Prasselnd in die dürre Frucht
Fällt sie, in des Speichers Räume,
In der Sparren dürre Bäume,
Und als wollte sie im Wehen
Mit sich fort der Erde Wucht
Reißen in gewaltger Flucht,
Wächst sie in des Himmels Höhen
Riesengroß. –
Hoffnungslos
Weicht der Mensch der Götterstärke,
Müßig sieht er seine Werke
Und bewundernd untergehen.

Leergebrannt
Ist die Stätte,
Wilder Stürme rauhes Bette.
In den öden Fensterhöhlen
Wohnt das Grauen,
Und des Himmels Wolken schauen
Hoch hinein.

Einen Blick
Nach dem Grabe
Seiner Habe
Sendet noch der Mensch zurück –
Greift fröhlich dann zum Wanderstabe.
Was Feuers Wut ihm auch geraubt,
Ein süßer Trost ist ihm geblieben:
Er zählt die Häupter seiner Lieben,
Und sieh! ihm fehlt kein teures Haupt.

In die Erd ists aufgenommen,
Glücklich ist die Form gefüllt;
Wirds auch schön zutage kommen,
Daß es Fleiß und Kunst vergilt?
    Wenn der Guß mißlang?

Cinders on the store-house frame,
And its drier stores, fall thick;
While kindling, blazing, mounting quick,
As though it would, at one fell sweep,
All that on the earth is found
Scatter wide in ruin round,
Swells the flame to heaven's blue deep,
With giant size.
Hope now dies.
Man must yield to Heaven's decrees.
Submissive, yet appalled, he sees
His fairest works in ashes sleep.

All burnt over
Is the place,
The storm's wild home. How changed its face!
In the empty, ruined wall
Dwells dark horror;
While heaven's clouds in shadow fall
Deep within.

One look,
In memory sad,
Of all he had,
The unhappy sufferer took, –
Then found his heart might yet be glad.
However hard his lot to bear,
His choicest treasures still remain:
He calls for each with anxious pain,
And every loved one's with him there.

To the earth it's now committed.
With success the mold is filled.
To skill and care alone's permitted
A perfect work with toil to build.
Is the casting right?

Wenn die Form zersprang?
Ach, vielleicht, indem wir hoffen,
Hat uns Unheil schon getroffen.

Dem dunkeln Schoß der heil'gen Erde
Vertrauen wir der Hände Tat,
Vertraut der Sämann seine Saat
Und hofft, daß sie entkeimen werde
Zum Segen, nach des Himmels Rat.
Noch köstlicheren Samen bergen
Wir trauernd in der Erde Schoß
Und hoffen, daß er aus den Särgen
Erblühen soll zu schönerm Los.

Von dem Dome
Schwer und bang
Tönt die Glocke
Grabgesang.
Ernst begleiten ihre Trauerschläge
Einen Wandrer auf dem letzten Wege.

Ach! die Gattin ists, die teure,
Ach! es ist die treue Mutter,
Die der schwarze Fürst der Schatten
Wegführt aus dem Arm des Gatten,
Aus der zarten Kinder Schar,
Die sie blühend ihm gebar,
Die sie an der treuen Brust
Wachsen sah mit Mutterlust —
Ach! des Hauses zarte Bande
Sind gelöst auf immerdar;
Denn sie wohnt im Schattenlande,
Die des Hauses Mutter war;
Denn es fehlt ihr treues Walten,
Ihre Sorge wacht nicht mehr;
An verwaister Stätte schalten
Wird die Fremde, liebeleer.

Is the mold yet tight?
Ah! while now with hope we wait,
Mischance, perhaps, attends its fate.

To the dark lap of mother earth
We now confide what we have made;
As in earth too the seed is laid,
In hope the seasons will give birth
To fruits that soon may be displayed.
And yet more precious seed we sow
With sorrow in the world's wide field;
And hope, though in the grave laid low,
A flower of heavenly hue 't will yield.

Slow and heavy
Hear it swell!
'Tis the solemn
Passing bell!
Sad we follow, with these sounds of woe,
Those who on this last, long journey go.

Alas! the wife, – it is the dear one, –
Ah, it is the faithful mother,
Whom the shadowy king of fear
Tears from all that life holds dear; –
From the husband, – from the young,
The tender blossoms, that have sprung
From their mutual, faithful love,
'Twas hers to nourish, guide, improve.
Ah! the chain which bound them all
Is for ever broken now;
She cannot hear their tender call,
Nor see them in affliction bow.
Her true affection guards no more;
Her watchful care wakes not again:
O'er all the once loved orphan's store
The indifferent stranger now must reign.

Bis die Glocke sich verkühlet,
Laßt die strenge Arbeit ruhn.
Wie im Laub der Vogel spielet,
Mag sich jeder gütlich tun.
　　Winkt der Sterne Licht,
　　Ledig aller Pflicht
Hört der Bursch die Vesper schlagen,
Meister muß sich immer plagen.


Munter fördert seine Schritte
Fern im wilden Forst der Wandrer
Nach der lieben Heimathütte.
Blökend ziehen heim die Schafe,
Und der Rinder
Breitgestirnte, glatte Scharen
Kommen brüllend,
Die gewohnten Ställe füllend.
Schwer herein
Schwankt der Wagen,
Kornbeladen;
Bunt von Farben
Auf den Garben
Liegt der Kranz,
Und das junge Volk der Schnitter
Fliegt zum Tanz.
Markt und Straße werden stiller,
Um des Lichts gesell'ge Flamme
Sammeln sich die Hausbewohner,
Und das Stadttor schließt sich knarrend.
Schwarz bedecket
Sich die Erde;
Doch den sichern Bürger schrecket
Nicht die Nacht,
Die den Bösen gräßlich wecket;
Denn das Auge des Gesetzes wacht.

Till the bell is safely cold,
May our heavy labor rest;
Free as the bird, by none controlled,
Each may do what pleases best.
  With approaching night,
  Twinkling stars are bright.
Vespers call the boys to play;
The master's toils end not with day.

Cheerful in the forest gloom,
The wanderer turns his weary steps
To his loved, though lowly home.
Bleating flocks draw near the fold;
And the herds,
Wide-horned, and smooth, slow-pacing come
Lowing from the hill,
The accustomed stall to fill.
Heavy rolls
Along the wagon,
Richly loaded.
On the sheaves,
With gayest leaves
They form the wreath;
And the youthful reapers dance
Upon the heath.
Street and market all are quiet,
And round each domestic light
Gathers now a circle fond,
While shuts the creaking city-gate.
Darkness hovers
O'er the earth.
Safety still each sleeper covers
As with light,
That the deeds of crime discovers;
For wakes the law's protecting might.

Heilge Ordnung, segenreiche
Himmelstochter, die das Gleiche
Frei und leicht und freudig bindet,
Die der Städte Bau gegründet,
Die herein von den Gefilden
Rief den ungesellgen Wilden,
Eintrat in der Menschen Hütten,
Sie gewöhnt zu sanften Sitten
Und das teuerste der Bande
Wob, den Trieb zum Vaterlande!

Tausend fleißge Hände regen,
Helfen sich in munterm Bund,
Und in feurigem Bewegen
Werden alle Kräfte kund.
Meister rührt sich und Geselle
In der Freiheit heil'gem Schutz;
Jeder freut sich seiner Stelle,
Bietet dem Verächter Trutz.
Arbeit ist des Bürgers Zierde,
Segen ist der Mühe Preis;
Ehrt den König seine Würde,
Ehret uns der Hände Fleiß.

Holder Friede,
Süße Eintracht,
Weilet, weilet
Freundlich über dieser Stadt!
Möge nie der Tag erscheinen,
Wo des rauhen Krieges Horden
Dieses stille Tal durchtoben;
Wo der Himmel,
Den des Abends sanfte Röte
Lieblich malt,
Von der Dörfer, von der Städte
Wildem Brande schrecklich strahlt!

Holy Order! rich with all
The gifts of Heaven, that best we call, –
Freedom, peace, and equal laws, –
Of common good the happy cause!
She the savage man has taught
What the arts of life have wrought;
Changed the rude hut to comfort, splendor,
And filled fierce hearts with feelings tender
And yet a dearer bond she wove, –
Our home, our country, taught to love.

A thousand active hands, combined
For mutual aid, with zealous heart,
In well apportioned labor find
Their power increasing with their art.
Master and workmen all agree,
Under sweet Freedom's holy care,
And each, content in his degree,
Warns every scorner to beware.
Labor is the poor man's pride, –
Success by toil alone is won.
Kings glory in possessions wide –
We glory in our work well done.

Gentle peace!
Sweet union!
Linger, linger,
Kindly over this our home!
Never may the day appear,
When the hordes of cruel war
Through this quiet vale shall rush;
When the sky,
With the evening's softened air,
Blushing red,
Shall reflect the frightful glare
Of burning towns in ruin dread.

Nun zerbrecht mir das Gebäude,
Seine Absicht hats erfüllt,
Daß sich Herz und Auge weide
An dem wohlgelungnen Bild.
   Schwingt den Hammer, schwingt,
   Bis der Mantel springt!
Wenn die Glock' soll auferstehen,
Muß die Form in Stücken gehen.


Der Meister kann die Form zerbrechen
Mit weiser Hand, zur rechten Zeit;
Doch wehe, wenn in Flammenbächen
Das glühnde Erz sich selbst befreit!
Blindwütend, mit des Donners Krachen,
Zersprengt es das geborstne Haus,
Und wie aus offnem Höllenrachen
Speit es Verderben zündend aus.
Wo rohe Kräfte sinnlos walten,
Da kann sich kein Gebild gestalten;
Wenn sich die Völker selbst befrein,
Da kann die Wohlfahrt nicht gedeihn.


Weh, wenn sich in dem Schoß der Städte
Der Feuerzunder still gehäuft,
Das Volk, zerreißend seine Kette,
Zur Eigenhilfe schrecklich greift!
Da zerret an der Glocke Strängen
Der Aufruhr, daß sie heulend schallt
Und, nur geweiht zu Friedensklängen,
Die Losung anstimmt zur Gewalt.


Freiheit und Gleichheit! hört man schallen,
Der ruhge Bürger greift zur Wehr,
Die Straßen füllen sich, die Hallen,

Now break up the useless mold:
Its only purpose is fulfilled.
May our eyes, well pleased, behold
A work to prove us not unskilled.
  Wield the hammer, wield,
  Till the frame shall yield!
That the bell to light may rise,
The form in thousand fragments flies.

The master may destroy the mold
With careful hand, and judgment wise.
But, woe! – in streams of fire, if rolled,
The glowing metal seek the skies!
Loud bursting with the clash of thunder,
It throws aloft the broken ground;
Like a volcano rends asunder,
And spreads in burning ruin round.
When reckless power by force prevails,
The reign of peace and art is o'er;
And when a mob e'en wrong assails,
The public welfare is no more.

Alas! when in the peaceful state
Conspiracies are darkly forming;
The oppressed no longer patient wait;
With fury every breast is storming.
Then whirls the bell with frequent clang;
And Uproar, with her howling voice,
Has changed the note, that peaceful rang,
To wild confusion's dreadful noise.

Freedom and equal rights they call, –
And peace gives way to sudden war;
The street is crowded, and the hall, –

Und Würgerbanden ziehn umher.
Da werden Weiber zu Hyänen
Und treiben mit Entsetzen Scherz;
Noch zuckend, mit des Panthers Zähnen,
Zerreißen sie des Feindes Herz.
Nichts Heiliges ist mehr, es lösen
Sich alle Bande frommer Scheu;
Der Gute räumt den Platz dem Bösen,
Und alle Laster walten frei.

Gefährlich ists, den Leu zu wecken,
Verderblich ist des Tigers Zahn;
Jedoch der schrecklichste der Schrecken,
Das ist der Mensch in seinem Wahn.
Weh denen, die dem Ewigblinden
Des Lichtes Himmelsfackel leihn!
Sie strahlt ihm nicht, sie kann nur zünden
Und äschert Städt und Länder ein.

Freude hat mir Gott gegeben!
Sehet! wie ein goldner Stern
Aus der Hülse, blank und eben,
Schält sich der metallne Kern.
Von dem Helm zum Kranz
Spielts wie Sonnenglanz,
Auch des Wappens nette Schilder
Loben den erfahrnen Bilder.

Herein! herein!
Gesellen alle, schließt den Reihen,
Daß wir die Glocke taufend weihen!
‚Concordia‘ soll ihr Name sein.
Zur Eintracht, zu herzinnigem Vereine
Versammle sie die liebende Gemeine.

And crime is unrestrained by law:
E'en woman, to a fury turning,
But mocks at every dreadful deed;
Against the hated madly burning,
With horrid joy she sees them bleed.
Now naught is sacred; – broken lies
Each holy law of honest worth;
The bad man rules, the good man flies,
And every vice walks boldly forth.

There's danger in the lion's wrath,
Destruction in the tiger's jaw;
But worse than death to cross the path
Of man, when passion is his law.
Woe, woe to those who strive to light
The torch of truth by passion's fire!
It guides not; – it but glares through night
To kindle freedom's funeral pyre.

God has given us joy tonight!
See how, like the golden grain
From the husk, all smooth and bright,
The shining metal now is ta'en!
From top to well formed rim,
Not a spot is dim;
E'en the motto, neatly raised,
Shows a skill may well be praised.

Around, around
Companions all, take your ground,
And name the bell with joy profound!
CONCORDIA is the word we've found
Most meet to express the harmonious sound
That calls to those in friendship bound.

Und dies sei fortan ihr Beruf,
Wozu der Meister sie erschuf:
Hoch überm niedern Erdenleben
Soll sie in blauem Himmelszelt,
Die Nachbarin des Donners, schweben
Und grenzen an die Sternenwelt,
Soll eine Stimme sein von oben,
Wie der Gestirne helle Schar,
Die ihren Schöpfer wandelnd loben
Und führen das bekränzte Jahr.
Nur ewigen und ernsten Dingen
Sei ihr metallner Mund geweiht,
Und stündlich mit den schnellen Schwingen
Berühr im Fluge sie die Zeit.
Dem Schicksal leihe sie die Zunge;
Selbst herzlos, ohne Mitgefühl,
Begleite sie mit ihrem Schwunge
Des Lebens wechselvolles Spiel.
Und wie der Klang im Ohr vergehet,
Der mächtig tönend ihr entschallt,
So lehre sie, daß nichts bestehet,
Daß alles Irdische verhallt.

Jetzo mit der Kraft des Stranges
Wiegt die Glock' mir aus der Gruft,
Daß sie in das Reich des Klanges
Steige, in die Himmelsluft.
  Ziehet, ziehet, hebt!
  Sie bewegt sich, schwebt.
Freude dieser Stadt bedeute,
Friede sei ihr erst Geläute.

Be this henceforth the destined end
To which the finished work we send
High over every meaner thing,
In the blue canopy of heaven,
Near to the thunder let it swing,
A neighbor to the stars be given.
Let its clear voice above proclaim,
With brightest troops of distant suns,
The praise of our Creator's name,
While round each circling season runs.
To solemn thoughts of heart-felt power
Let its deep note full oft invite,
And tell, with every passing hour,
Of hastening time's unceasing flight.
Still let it mark the course of fate;
Its cold, unsympathizing voice
Attend on every changing state
Of human passions, griefs, and joys.
And as the mighty sound it gives
Dies gently on the listening ear,
We feel how quickly all that lives
Must change, and fade, and disappear.

Now, lads, join your strength around!
Lift the bell to upper air!
And in the kingdom wide of sound
Once placed, we'll leave it there.
    All together! heave!
    Its birth-place see it leave! –
Joy to all within its bound!
Peace its first, its latest sound!

*Henry Wadsworth Longfellow*

*Adalbert von Chamisso*

## DIE WEIBER VON WINSPERG

Der erste Hohenstaufen, der König Konrad, lag
Mit Heeresmacht vor Winsperg seit manchem langen Tag;
Der Welfe war geschlagen, noch wehrte sich das Nest,
Die unverzagten Städter, die hielten es noch fest.

Der Hunger kam, der Hunger! das ist ein scharfer Dorn;
Nun suchten sie die Gnade, nun fanden sie den Zorn.
„Ihr habt mir hier erschlagen gar manchen Degen wert,
Und öffnet ihr die Tore, so trifft euch doch das Schwert."

Da sind die Weiber kommen: „Und muß es also sein,
Gewährt uns freien Abzug, wir sind vom Blute rein."
Da hat sich vor den Armen des Helden Zorn gekühlt,
Da hat ein sanft Erbarmen im Herzen er gefühlt.

„Die Weiber mögen abziehn, und jede habe frei,
Was sie vermag zu tragen und ihr das Liebste sei!
Laßt ziehn mit ihrer Bürde sie ungehindert fort!
Das ist des Königs Meinung, das ist des Königs Wort."

Und als der frühe Morgen im Osten kaum gegraut,
Da hat ein seltnes Schauspiel vom Lager man geschaut;
Es öffnet leise, leise sich das bedrängte Tor,
Es schwankt ein Zug von Weibern mit schwerem Schritt hervor.

Tief beugt die Last sie nieder, die auf dem Nacken ruht,
Sie tragen ihre Ehherrn, das ist ihr liebstes Gut.
„Halt an die argen Weiber!" ruft drohend mancher Wicht;
Der Kanzler spricht bedeutsam: „Das war die Meinung nicht."

## THE WOMEN OF WEINSPERG

King Conrad Hohenstaufen with mighty forces lay
Before the town of Weinsperg, for many a weary day.
Although the Guelf was beaten, the town's defense was strong,
The citizens, undaunted, held out in it for long.

The hunger came, the hunger that is a pointed thorn.
When now they looked for mercy, they found but wrathful scorn.
"The bravest of my fighters you slew to my regret.
And should the gates be opened, the sword shall strike you yet!"

But then there came the women: "If thus it has to be,
Let us depart in safety; from blood our hands are free."
The hero's wrath abated on seeing them distressed,
He felt a gentle pity upwelling in his breast.

"In peace may go the women, and of the goods they boast,
Each take what she can carry, and what she treasures most;
And let them, with their burden, go hence quite undeterred!
For this is my opinion, and this my royal word."

And barely had the morning lit up the eastern sky,
When from the camp was witnessed what rarely meets the eye:
A gate was slowly opened, that from the city led,
A swaying line of women came forth with heavy tread.

Bent deep beneath the burden, that on their shoulders pressed,
They carried each her husband, the treasure each loved best.
"Hold back the wily women!" With threats the air is rent.
The chancellor says, important: "'Tis not as it was meant."

Da hat, wie ers vernommen, der fromme Herr gelacht:
„Und war es nicht die Meinung, sie habens gut gemacht;
Gesprochen ist gesprochen, das Königswort besteht,
Und zwar von keinem Kanzler zerdeutelt und zerdreht."

But when he heard the tidings, the king laughed out with glee:
"Although 'twas not the meaning, they acted splendidly!"
What's said, is said for ever, the royal word persists.
No chancellor shall, moreover, give turns to it and twists.

*Helen Kurz Roberts*

## DER SOLDAT

Es geht bei gedämpfter Trommel Klang,
Wie weit noch die Stätte, der Weg wie lang!
O käm er zur Ruh und wär es vorbei!
Ich glaub', es bricht mir das Herz entzwei.

Ich hab' in der Welt nur ihn geliebt,
Nur ihn, dem jetzt man den Tod doch gibt.
Bei klingendem Spiele wird paradiert,
Dazu bin ich auch kommandiert.

Da schaut er auf zum letzten Mal
In Gottes Sonne freudigen Strahl;
Nun binden sie ihm die Augen zu –
Dir schenke Gott die ewige Ruh!

Es haben die Neun wohl angelegt,
Acht Kugeln haben vorbeigefegt;
Sie zitterten alle vor Jammer und Schmerz,
Ich aber, ich traf ihn mitten in's Herz.

## THE SOLDIER

We march to the sound of muffled drum,
How long the road, how far we must come!
O were it but over, O were he at rest!
I think, my heart will break in my breast.

In all the world I loved but him,
Him whom to death they now condemn.
With fife and bugle we pass in review,
And I am part of the escort too.

Now comes his last, his only chance
To give God's sun a farewell glance,
And now the blindfold, blessed release,
May God vouchsafe you eternal peace!

Nine rifles carefully are aimed,
Eight bullets past his head have flamed;
With fear and terror their hearts did pound,
My bullet alone his heart has found.

*Heinz Norden*

## DAS RIESENSPIELZEUG

Burg Niedeck ist im Elsaß, der Sage wohl bekannt,
Die Höhe, wo vor Zeiten die Burg der Riesen stand;
Sie selbst ist nun verfallen, die Stätte wüst und leer,
Du fragest nach den Riesen, du findest sie nicht mehr.

Einst kam das Riesenfräulein aus jener Burg hervor,
Erging sich sonder Wartung und spielend vor dem Tor
Und stieg hinab den Abhang bis in das Tal hinein,
Neugierig zu erkunden, wie's unten möchte sein.

Mit wen'gen raschen Schritten durchkreuzte sie den Wald,
Erreichte gegen Haslach das Land der Menschen bald,
Und Städte dort und Dörfer und das bestellte Feld
Erschienen ihren Augen gar eine fremde Welt.

Wie jetzt zu ihren Füßen sie spähend niederschaut,
Bemerkt sie einen Bauer, der seinen Acker baut;
Es kriecht das kleine Wesen einher so sonderbar,
Es glitzert in der Sonne der Pflug so blank und klar.

,,Ei! Artig Spielding!'' ruft sie, ,,das nehm' ich mit nach Haus!''
Sie knieet nieder, spreitet behend ihr Tüchlein aus
Und feget mit den Händen, was sich da alles regt,
Zu Haufen in das Tüchlein, das sie zusammenschlägt,

Und eilt mit freud'gen Sprüngen, man weiß, wie Kinder sind,
Zur Burg hinan und suchet den Vater auf geschwind:
,,Ei, Vater, lieber Vater, ein Spielding wunderschön!
So Allerliebstes sah ich noch nie auf unsern Höh'n.''

Der Alte saß am Tische und trank den kühlen Wein,
Er schaut sie an behaglich, er fragt das Töchterlein:

## THE GIANT'S TOY

The Niedeck in Alsatia is known to country lore,
The height on which a castle of giants stood before;
The hall now lies in ruins, deserted, bare the ground,
The giants, should you seek them, are no more to be found.

One day a giant maiden went forth from the estate,
She strolled without attendance and played before the gate,
The slope she then descended towards the vale below;
What life might be down yonder was what she longed to know.

With few and rapid paces she crossed the forest span
And near a place called Hasslach she reached the realm of man,
The townships there, the hamlets, the cultivated field,
Her eyes esteemed them wondrous, an unknown world revealed.

On looking at her feet then, what closer search might yield,
She notices a peasant about to plough his field.
The little creature crawling affords so strange a sight,
The ploughshare in the sunlight is flashing clear and bright.

"Oh, what a lovely plaything," she shouts, "I'll take you home."
She nimbly spreads her kerchief and kneeling on the loam
She gathers all together what stirs upon the ground
And heaps it on her kerchief which then she wraps around.

With joyous leaps she hastens, you all know children's ways,
Back home, and to her father she runs at once and says:
"O father, dearest father, a toy, a sheer delight,
Such lovely thing I never have seen upon our height!"

The old man sat at table and sipped a vintage mild;
He looks at her complacent and then he asks the child:

„Was Zappeliges bringst du in deinem Tuch herbei?
Du hüpfest ja vor Freuden; laß sehen, was es sei."

Sie spreitet aus das Tüchlein und fängt behutsam an,
Den Bauer aufzustellen, den Pflug und das Gespann;
Wie alles auf dem Tische sie zierlich aufgebaut,
So klatscht sie in die Hände und springt und jubelt laut.

Der Alte wird gar ernsthaft und wiegt sein Haupt und spricht:
„Was hast du angerichtet? Das ist kein Spielzeug nicht!
Wo du es hergenommen, da trag es wieder hin,
Der Bauer ist kein Spielzeug, was kommt dir in den Sinn?

Sollst gleich und ohne Murren erfüllen mein Gebot;
Denn wäre nicht der Bauer, so hättest du kein Brot;
Es sprießt der Stamm der Riesen aus Bauernmark hervor,
Der Bauer ist kein Spielzeug, da sei uns Gott davor!"

Burg Niedeck ist im Elsaß, der Sage wohl bekannt,
Die Höhe, wo vor Zeiten die Burg der Riesen stand;
Sie selbst ist nun verfallen, die Stätte wüst und leer,
Und fragst du nach den Riesen, du findest sie nicht mehr.

"What wriggles in your kerchief, what have you brought to me?
You jump about with pleasure, now show what it may be."

She spreads her little kerchief and carefully she now
Sets up at first the peasant, and then the team and plough.
When all upon the table is built up prettily
She claps her hands, she dances and shouts aloud with glee.

The old man's face grows solemn, he shakes his head to say:
"Whatever are you adoing, 'tis not a thing for play!
From where you brought it hither, you'll take it back with care.
A peasant is no plaything, what made you think he were?

"At once obey my bidding, no further word be said,
For if there were no peasant, you lacked the daily bread;
The giants rose from peasants, to them we are akin;
The peasant is no plaything, may God forbid such sin!"

The Niedeck, in Alsatia, is known to country lore,
The height on which a castle of giants stood before;
The hall now lies in ruins, deserted, bare the ground,
The giants, should you seek them, are no more to be found.

*Helen Kurz Roberts*

## DAS SCHLOSS BONCOURT

Ich träum als Kind mich zurücke
Und schüttle mein greises Haupt;
Wie sucht ihr mich heim, ihr Bilder,
Die lang ich vergessen geglaubt?

Hoch ragt aus schatt'gen Gehegen
Ein schimmerndes Schloß hervor,
Ich kenne die Türme, die Zinnen,
Die steinerne Brücke, das Tor.

Es schauen vom Wappenschilde
Die Löwen so traulich mich an,
Ich grüße die alten Bekannten
Und eile den Burghof hinan.

Dort liegt die Sphinx am Brunnen,
Dort grünt der Feigenbaum,
Dort, hinter diesen Fenstern,
Verträumt ich den ersten Traum.

Ich tret' in die Burgkapelle
Und suche des Ahnherrn Grab;
Dort ist's, dort hängt vom Pfeiler
Das alte Gewaffen herab.

## THE CASTLE OF BONCOURT

I dream I am back in my childhood
And shake my greying head;
They haunt me anew, the visions,
I long thought forgotten, nay, dead.

A gleaming castle is rising
Above a woodland estate;
I know the gables, the towers,
The stone bridge as well as the gate.

The lions that flank the escutcheon
Look down with friendly regard,
I greet them, the old acquaintance,
And hasten across the yard.

There lies the sphinx by the fountain,
And there stands the figtree in leaf,
And there, behind those windows,
I first knew joy and grief.

I enter the castle's chapel
And look for the ancestor's tomb;
'Tis there and above on the pillar
The ancient weapons loom.

Noch lesen umflort die Augen
Die Züge der Inschrift nicht,
Wie hell durch die bunten Scheiben
Das Licht darüber auch bricht.


So stehst du, o Schloß meiner Väter,
Mir treu und fest in dem Sinn,
Und bist von der Erde verschwunden,
Der Pflug geht über dich hin.


Sei fruchtbar, o teurer Boden,
Ich segne dich mild und gerührt
Und segn' ihn zwiefach, wer immer
Den Pflug nun über dich führt.


Ich aber will auf mich rafl
Mein Saitenspiel in der Hand,
Die Weiten der Erde durchschweifen
Und singen von Land zu Land.

The tear-dimmed eye cannot read yet
The lines that are carved on the grave,
Although through the painted windows
Bright light is flooding the nave.


And thus, O home of my fathers,
Thou'll stand in my heart. I vow,
Hast vanished from the earth though,
And over thee passes the plough.


O cherished soil, be fertile!
I bless thee tenderly
And twofold be blessed whoever
Is driving the plough over thee.


But I shall forgather my powers
And taking the lute in my hand
Will roam through the world's wide spaces
And sing from land to land.

*Helen Kurz Roberts*

*Ludwig Uhland*

## BERTRAN DE BORN

Droben auf dem schroffen Steine
Raucht in Trümmern Autafort,
Und der Burgherr steht gefesselt
Vor des Königs Zelte dort:
,,Kamst du, der mit Schwert und Liedern
Aufruhr trug von Ort zu Ort,
Der die Kinder aufgewiegelt
Gegen ihres Vaters Wort?

Steht vor mir, der sich gerühmet
In vermeßner Prahlerei,
Daß ihm nie mehr als die Hälfte
Seines Geistes nötig sei?
Nun der halbe dich nicht rettet,
Ruf den ganzen doch herbei,
Daß er neu dein Schloß dir baue,
Deine Ketten brech entzwei!‘‘

,,Wie du sagst, mein Herr und König,
Steht vor dir Bertran de Born,
Der mit einem Lied entflammte
Perigord und Ventadorn,
Der dem mächtigen Gebieter
Stets im Auge war ein Dorn,
Dem zu Liebe Königskinder
Trugen ihres Vaters Zorn.

Deine Tochter saß im Saale,
Festlich, eines Herzogs Braut,

### BERTRAN DE BORN

Autafort, in ruins, smoulders
Yonder on that rocky dent
And its lord, he stands in fetters
There before the royal tent:
"Hast thou come who spread rebellion
Everywhere with song and sword,
Thou who hast induced my children
To defy their father's word?

"Stands before me he who boasted
In vainglorious conceit
That, whatever be the hazard,
Half his spirit would be meet?
Call upon the whole to save thee
Since the half has tried in vain,
Make it build anew thy castle,
Let it break thy heavy chain!"

"As thou say'st, my king and master,
Here I stand, Bertran de Born,
Who with song has set on fire
Perigord and Ventadorn,
Whom his mighty ruler ever
Thought a thorn within his side,
For whose sake the royal children
Bore their father's wrath with pride.

"In the festive hall, your daughter,
Pledged to wed a duke, held sway,

Und da sang vor ihr mein Bote,
Dem ein Lied ich anvertraut,
Sang, was einst ihr Stolz gewesen,
Ihres Dichters Sehnsuchtlaut,
Bis ihr leuchtend Brautgeschmeide
Ganz von Tränen war betaut.

Aus des Ölbaums Schlummerschatten
Fuhr dein bester Sohn empor,
Als mit zorngen Schlachtgesängen
Ich bestürmen ließ sein Ohr.
Schnell war ihm das Roß gegürtet,
Und ich trug das Banner vor,
Jenem Todespfeil entgegen,
Der ihn traf vor Montforts Tor.

Blutend lag er mir im Arme;
Nicht der scharfe, kalte Stahl –
Daß er sterb in deinem Fluche,
Das war seines Sterbens Qual.
Strecken wollt er dir die Rechte
Über Meer, Gebirg und Tal;
Als er deine nicht erreichet,
Drückt' er meine noch einmal.

Da, wie Autafort dort oben,
Ward gebrochen meine Kraft;
Nicht die ganze, nicht die halbe,
Blieb mir, Saite nicht, noch Schaft.
Leicht hast du den Arm gebunden,
Seit der Geist mir liegt in Haft;
Nur zu einem Trauerliede
Hatt er sich noch aufgerafft.''

When the page I had entrusted
With a poem sang my lay,
Sang her poet's ardent longing
That had been her secret pride,
Till her shining tears in glitter
With her bridal jewels vied.

"From the shade of olive branches
Rose the son thy heart held dear,
When with fiery songs of battle
I assailed his willing ear.
Speedily his steed was girded
And I bore his flag and crest,
Led him to the gate of Montfort
Where that arrow pierced his breast.

"In my arms I held him, bleeding;
Not the pointed steel felt he, –
But to die, thy curse upon him,
Was his dying agony.
And his hand, stretched out with longing,
Tried to span the hill and dell;
When he could not clasp his father's,
Mine he pressed in sad farewell.

"Then, like Autafort up yonder,
Broken was my strength, Mylord;
Whole or half, I since had neither,
Not the lute and not the sword.
Easily my arm was shackled
Since my spirit drags a chain,
And this song, to voice my sorrow,
Is the last it will attain."

Und der König senkt die Stirne:
„Meinen Sohn hast du verführt,
Hast der Tochter Herz verzaubert,
Hast auch meines nun gerührt.
Nimm die Hand, du Freund des Toten,
Die, verzeihend, ihm gebührt!
Weg die Fesseln! Deines Geistes
Hab ich einen Hauch verspürt."

And the king, his forehead lowered:
"Thou enticed my bravest son,
Cast a spell upon my daughter,
And hast moved my heart anon.
Take my hand, with it the pardon
Due to him thou eased in death!
Loose his fetters! Of thy spirit
I, myself, have felt a breath."

*Helen Kurz Roberts*

## DES SÄNGERS FLUCH

Es stand in alten Zeiten ein Schloß, so hoch und hehr;
Weit glänzt es über die Lande bis an das blaue Meer,
Und rings von duftgen Gärten ein blütenreicher Kranz,
Drin sprangen frische Brunnen in Regenbogenglanz.

Dort saß ein stolzer König, an Land und Siegen reich,
·Er saß auf seinem Throne so finster und so bleich;
Denn was er sinnt, ist Schrecken, und was er blickt, ist Wut,
Und was er spricht, ist Geißel, und was er schreibt, ist Blut.

Einst zog nach diesem Schlosse ein edles Sängerpaar,
Der ein in goldnen Locken, der andre grau von Haar.
Der Alte mit der Harfe, der saß auf schmuckem Roß,
Es schritt ihm frisch zur Seite der blühende Genoß.

Der Alte sprach zum Jungen: ,,Nun sei bereit, mein Sohn!
Denk unsrer tiefsten Lieder, stimm an den vollsten Ton!
Nimm alle Kraft zusammen, die Lust und auch den Schmerz!
Es gilt uns heut, zu rühren des Königs steinern Herz.''

Schon stehn die beiden Sänger im hohen Säulensaal,
Und auf dem Throne sitzen der König und sein Gemahl,
Der König furchtbar prächtig, wie blut'ger Nordlichtschein,
Die Königin süß und milde, als blickte Vollmond drein.

Da schlug der Greis die Saiten, er schlug sie wundervoll,
Daß reicher, immer reicher der Klang zum Ohre schwoll;
Dann strömte himmlisch helle des Jünglings Stimme vor,
Des Alten Sang dazwischen wie dumpfer Geisterchor.

Sie singen von Lenz und Liebe, von selger goldner Zeit,
Von Freiheit, Männerwürde, von Treu und Heiligkeit,

## THE CURSE OF THE BARD

In byegone times there towered a castle loftily:
It shone far o'er the country and to the deep blue sea.
Around it fragrant gardens, like flower garlands lay
Wherein the cooling fountains sent up their rainbow spray.

There sat a proud king, boasting of land and victory,
His visage pale and scowling, he reigned in infamy;
His every thought is terror, his eyes with fury flame,
The words he speaks are scourges, with blood he signs his name.

Once journeyed to this castle of bards a noble pair.
The one with golden ringlets, the other gray of hair;
A harp the old one carried, a noble steed he rode,
And by his side, light-footed, his young companion strode.

The old spake to the younger: "Make ready, son, recall
The songs that are most stirring, by fullest tone enthrall!
Forgather all your powers, let joy and sorrow ring!
Today we aim at moving the stone heart of the king!"

And now the bards have entered the lofty, pillared hall.
The king and queen are seated within the sight of all,
The king, resplendent, awesome, like blood-red northern light,
The queen so sweet and gentle, like moonbeams in the night.

The old man struck the chords now 'twas wonderful to hear
And richer, always richer, the sounds assailed the ear,
Then clear, like bells of heaven, rang out the young man's tone,
The old one's intermingling, a hollow, ghostly drone.

They sing of love and springtime, the golden days of glee,
Of liberty and honor, of faith and sanctity;

Sie singen von allem Süßen, was Menschenbrust durchbebt,
Sie singen von allem Hohen, was Menschenherz erhebt.


Die Höflingsschar im Kreise verlernet jeden Spott,
Des Königs trotzge Krieger, sie beugen sich vor Gott;
Die Königin, zerflossen in Wehmut und in Lust,
Sie wirft den Sängern nieder die Rose von ihrer Brust.


„Ihr habt mein Volk verführet; verlockt ihr nun mein Weib?"
Der König schreit es wütend, er bebt am ganzen Leib;
Er wirft sein Schwert, das blitzend des Jünglings Brust durchdringt,
Draus statt der goldnen Lieder ein Blutstrahl hoch aufspringt.


Und wie vom Sturm zerstoben ist all der Hörer Schwarm.
Der Jüngling hat verröchelt in seines Meisters Arm;
Der schlägt um ihn den Mantel und setzt ihn auf das Roß,
Er bind't ihn aufrecht feste, verläßt mit ihm das Schloß.


Doch vor dem hohen Tore, da hält der Sängergreis,
Da faßt er seine Harfe, sie, aller Harfen Preis,
An einer Marmorsäule, da hat er sie zerschellt;
Dann ruft er, daß es schaurig durch Schloß und Gärten gellt:


„Weh euch, ihr stolzen Hallen! Nie töne süßer Klang
Durch eure Räume wieder, nie Saite noch Gesang,
Nein, Seufzer nur und Stöhnen und scheuer Sklavenschritt,
Bis euch zu Schutt und Moder der Rachegeist zertritt!


Weh euch, ihr duftgen Gärten im holden Maienlicht!
Euch zeig ich dieses Toten entstelltes Angesicht,
Daß ihr darob verdorret, daß jeder Quell versiegt,
Daß ihr in künftgen Tagen versteint, verödet liegt.


Weh dir, verruchter Mörder, du Fluch des Sängertums!
Umsonst sei all dein Ringen nach Kränzen blutgen Ruhms!

They sing of what is sweetest, that which the heart likes best,
They sing of what is noblest, and swells the human breast.

The courtiers all assembled forget to jeer and prod,
The king's defiant warriors, they bow before their God.
The queen, whose heart is melting in ecstasy and pain,
The rose from off her bosom she throweth to the twain.

"You have enticed my people, my wife do now you charm?"
The king calls out, all shaking with fury and alarm;
He throws his sword which pierces the young man's breast and woe!
Instead of golden singing, the blood is spurting low.

The listeners are scattered as if by icy blast;
Supported by his master, the youth has breathed his last;
He cloaks him in his mantle, and upright on his steed
He binds him fast, thus leaving the scene of this foul deed.

Before the mighty gateway the old bard comes to rest,
And there his harp he seizes, of all the harps the best,
Against a marble pillar he shatters it and calls
So that it awesome echoes, through garden and through halls.

"Be cursed, you stately castle! may nevermore sweet tongue
Resound through your apartments, no harping and no song,
But only sighing, moaning, the tread of shy distrust,
Till the avenging spirit has crushed you into dust!

"Be cursed, you fragrant gardens, now bathing in the light!
These dead, disfigured features I offer to your sight,
Would that thereby they withered, that every spring ran dry,
So that you might in future a stony wasteland lie.

"And woe to you, vile slayer, you curse of poetry!
In vain be all your striving for crowns of victory!

Dein Name sei vergessen, in ewge Nacht getaucht,
Sei wie ein letztes Röcheln in leere Luft verhaucht!"

Der Alte hats gerufen, der Himmel hats gehört.
Die Mauern liegen nieder, die Hallen sind zerstört;
Noch eine hohe Säule zeugt von verschwundner Pracht;
Auch diese, schon geborsten, kann stürzen über Nacht.

Und rings statt duftger Gärten ein ödes Heideland,
Kein Baum verstreuet Schatten, kein Quell durchdringt den Sand,
Des Königs Namen meldet kein Lied, kein Heldenbuch;
Versunken und vergessen! Das ist des Sängers Fluch.

Your name, engulfed in darkness, forgotten everywhere
Shall like a last death rattle be spilled upon the air!"

And what the old man shouted, in heaven it was heard;
The walls have fallen crumbling, the pillared halls are bared;
A lonely, lofty column attests to former might,
And this already cracking may tumble overnight.

Instead of fragrant gardens deserted heatherland,
No tree to scatter shadow, no spring to pierce the sand.
The king's name is recorded in neither song nor verse,
Forsaken and forgotten, that is the bard's old curse.

*Helen Kurz Roberts*

## DAS SCHLOSS AM MEER

Hast du das Schloß gesehen,
Das hohe Schloß am Meer?
Golden und rosig wehen
Die Wolken drüber her.

Es möchte sich niederneigen
In die spiegelklare Flut;
Es möchte streben und steigen
In der Abendwolken Glut.

„Wohl hab ich es gesehen,
Das hohe Schloß am Meer.
Und den Mond darüber stehen
Und Nebel weit umher."

Der Wind und des Meeres Wallen,
Gaben sie frischen Klang?
Vernahmst du aus den Hallen
Saiten und Festgesang?

„Die Winde, die Wogen alle
Lagen in tiefer Ruh;
Einem Klagelied aus der Halle
Hört ich mit Tränen zu."

Sahest du oben gehen
Den König und sein Gemahl?
Der roten Mäntel Wehen,
Der goldnen Kronen Strahl?

Führten sie nicht mit Wonne
Eine schöne Jungfrau dar,

## THE CASTLE BY THE SEA

"And hast thou seen it shining,
The castle that stands by the sea?
Rose-clouds with golden lining
Pass over it leisurely.

It longs to be bending and diving
Into the crystal flow,
It longs to be stretching and striving
To rise to the evening glow." –

"Aye well, I saw it shining
The castle that stands by the sea.
A pallid moon was declining
And mist lay over the lea." –

The wind and the waves, were they singing
Their clear, strong melody?
And were the halls not ringing
With harping and festive glee?" –

"The wind and the waves were lying
Motionless under the skies;
To a tune, as mournful as sighing,
I harkened, tears in my eyes." –

"And did'st thou espy, I wonder,
In billowing, purple gowns,
The king and the queen up yonder
And the glitter of golden crowns?

Were they not leading with pleasure
A maiden surpassing fair?

Herrlich wie eine Sonne,
Strahlend im goldnen Haar?

„Wohl sah ich die Eltern beide,
Ohne der Kronen Licht,
Im schwarzen Trauerkleide;
Die Jungfrau sah ich nicht."

The golden sun would treasure
The glory of her hair." –

"Without their crowns adorning
I saw the royal pair,
In a garb of deepest mourning,
The maiden was not there!"

*Helen Kurz Roberts*

## SCHWÄBISCHE KUNDE

Als Kaiser Rotbart lobesam
Zum heil'gen Land gezogen kam,
Da mußt er mit dem frommen Heer
Durch ein Gebirge, wüst und leer.
Daselbst erhub sich große Not,
Viel Steine gabs und wenig Brot,
Und mancher deutsche Reitersmann
Hat dort den Trunk sich abgetan.
Den Pferden wars so schwach im Magen,
Fast mußt der Reiter die Mähre tragen.
Nun war ein Herr aus Schwabenland,
Von hohem Wuchs und starker Hand,
Des Rößlein war so krank und schwach,
Er zog es nur am Zaume nach:
Er hätt es nimmer aufgegeben,
Und kostets ihn das eigne Leben.
So blieb er bald ein gutes Stück
Hinter dem Heereszug zurück;
Da sprengten plötzlich in die Quer
Fünfzig türkische Reiter daher:
Die huben an auf ihn zu schießen,
Nach ihm zu werfen mit den Spießen.
Der wackre Schwabe forcht' sich nit,
Ging seines Weges Schritt vor Schritt,
Ließ sich den Schild mit Pfeilen spicken
Und tät nur spöttlich um sich blicken,
Bis einer, dem die Zeit zu lang,
Auf ihn den krummen Säbel schwang.
Da wallt dem Deutschen auch sein Blut,
Er trifft des Türken Pferd so gut,
Er haut ihm ab mit einem Streich
Die beiden Vorderfüß zugleich.

## SWABIAN TIDINGS

When Barbarossa, praised be he,
Had reached the Holy Land, needs be
The pious host he led must fare
Through mountains, desolate and bare.
Thereat great dearth reared up its head,
For stones were plenty, not so bread,
And many German horsemen w re
Compelled to give up drinking there.
The nags, with empty maws, felt weak,
The rider almost bore the steed.
There was a knight from Swabian land,
Of stately build and strong of hand,
Whose horse was feeble and in pain,
He only led it by the rein;
Yet though his life might be at stake,
His steed he never would forsake.
And so he stayed, because of it,
Behind the host a goodly bit.
Then suddenly, across his course,
Came fifty of the Turkish horse;
They started shooting, then closed in,
And each one threw his javelin.
The Swabian brave, without dismay,
Continued slowly on his way,
He let their arrows spike his shield
And only sneered quite unconcealed,
Till one, who in particular
Was hasty, swung his scimitar.
At that the German's pulse does throb
He squarely hits the Turkish cob,
And with a single stroke, well done,
Lops off its forelegs, both in one.

Als er das Tier zu Fall gebracht,
Da faßt er erst sein Schwert mit Macht,
Er schwingt es auf des Reiters Kopf,
Haut durch bis auf den Sattelknopf,
Haut auch den Sattel noch zu Stücken
Und tief noch in des Pferdes Rücken;
Zur Rechten sieht man wie zur Linken
Einen halben Türken heruntersinken.
Da packt die andern kalter Graus:
Sie fliehen in alle Welt hinaus,
Und jedem ists, als würd ihm mitten
Durch Kopf und Leib hindurchgeschnitten.
Drauf kam des Wegs 'ne Christenschar,
Die auch zurückgeblieben war;
Die sahen nun mit gutem Bedacht,
Was Arbeit unser Held gemacht.
Von denen hats der Kaiser vernommen.
Der ließ den Schwaben vor sich kommen;
Er sprach: ,,Sag an, mein Ritter wert!
Wer hat dich solche Streich gelehrt?"
Der Held bedacht sich nicht zu lang:
,,Die Streiche sind bei uns im Schwang,
Sie sind bekannt im ganzen Reiche,
Man nennt sie halt nur Schwabenstreiche."

Now once the horse was down, the knight
He swings his sword with all his might
And, standing o'er the Turk astraddle,
He cleaves him through unto the saddle;
The saddle too he cuts and slits
And deep the horse's back he hits;
To right and left is seen afalling
Just half a Turk, a sight appalling.
Cold terror grips the rest, they flee
To anywhere, ingloriously,
And each one feels as though the coup
Has cleft his head and trunk in two.
Just then some Christians chanced that way
Who too had suffered some delay;
They saw, with circumspect delight,
What splendid work had done our knight.
From them the emperor had report.
He bade the knight to come to court.
"My brave, who taught thee," thus he spoke,
"To halve a man with just one stroke?"
At this our hero only laughs:
"We Swabians all do things by halves.
'Tis also said by those that matter,
We make a hash of any matter."

*Helen Kurz Roberts*

## DER WIRTIN TÖCHTERLEIN

Es zogen drei Burschen wohl über den Rhein,
Bei einer Frau Wirtin da kehrten sie ein.

„Frau Wirtin! hat Sie gut Bier und Wein?
Wo hat Sie ihr schönes Töchterlein?"

„Mein Bier und Wein ist frisch und klar.
Mein Töchterlein liegt auf der Totenbahr."

Und als sie traten zur Kammer hinein,
Da lag sie in einem schwarzen Schrein.

Der erste, der schlug den Schleier zurück
Und schaute sie an mit traurigem Blick:

„Ach! lebtest du noch, du schöne Maid!
Ich würde dich lieben von dieser Zeit."

Der zweite deckte den Schleier zu
Und kehrte sich ab und weinte dazu:

„Ach! daß du liegst auf der Totenbahr!
Ich hab dich geliebet so manches Jahr."

Der dritte hub ihn wieder sogleich
Und küßte sie an den Mund so bleich:

„Dich liebt ich immer, dich lieb ich noch heut
Und werde dich lieben in Ewigkeit."

## MINE HOSTESS' DAUGHTER

Three lads ajourneying crossed the Rhine,
They called at an inn, they well knew its sign.

"Mine hostess, hast thou good ale and wine?
Where hast thou thy daughter so fair and fine?"

"My ale and wine are fresh and clear,
My daughter is lying upon her bier!"

And when they entered the room behind,
They saw her there in a coffin confined.

The first one lifted the veil with a sigh,
Looked down on her with a mournful eye:

"Fair maiden, would that thou wert not gone!
I should have loved thee from this day on."

The second let drop the veil in place
And turned away his tear-stained face.

"Alack that thou liest upon a bier!
For I have loved thee for many a year."

The third one at once threw back the veil
And kissed her on her mouth so pale:

"I love thee today as I loved thee afore
And I shall love thee evermore!"

*Helen Kurz Roberts*

## DER GUTE KAMERAD

Ich hatt einen Kameraden,
Einen bessern findst du nit.
Die Trommel schlug zum Streite,
Er ging an meiner Seite
In gleichem Schritt und Tritt.

Eine Kugel kam geflogen;
Gilt's mir oder gilt es dir?
Ihn hat es weggerissen,
Er liegt mir vor den Füßen,
Als wär's ein Stück von mir.

Will mir die Hand noch reichen,
Derweil ich eben lad:
Kann dir die Hand nicht geben;
Bleib du im ew'gen Leben,
Mein guter Kamerad!

## THE FAITHFUL COMRADE

I had a faithful comrade,
No better can be found.
To battle drums were guiding,
Beside me he was striding,
In step we paced the ground.

A bullet came aflying,
Is it meant for thee or me?
'Tis he was felled and dying,
Now at my feet he's lying,
As if a part of me.

His hand is stretched towards me,
Just as I load anew.
"I cannot give my hand to thee,
In after-life be friend to me,
My comrade brave and true."

*Helen Kurz Roberts*

*Friedrich Rückert*

## CHIDHER

Chidher, der ewig junge, sprach:
Ich fuhr an einer Stadt vorbei,
Ein Mann im Garten Früchte brach;
Ich fragte, seit wann die Stadt hier sei?
Er sprach, und pflückte die Früchte fort:
,,Die Stadt steht ewig an diesem Ort
Und wird so stehen ewig fort.'' –
Und aber nach fünfhundert Jahren
Kam ich desselbigen Wegs gefahren.

Da fand ich keine Spur der Stadt;
Ein einsamer Schäfer blies die Schalmei,
Die Herde weidete Laub und Blatt;
Ich fragte, wie lang ist die Stadt vorbei?
Er sprach, und blies auf dem Rohre fort:
,,Das eine wächst, wenn das andere dorrt;
Das ist mein ewiger Weideort.'' –
Und aber nach fünfhundert Jahren
Kam ich desselbigen Wegs gefahren.

Da fand ich ein Meer, das Wellen schlug,
Ein Schiffer warf die Netze frei;
Und als er ruhte vom schweren Zug,
Fragt ich, seit wann das Meer hier sei?
Er sprach und lachte meinem Wort:
,,So lang, als schäumen die Wellen dort,
Fischt man und fischt man in diesem Port.'' –
Und aber nach fünfhundert Jahren
Kam ich desselbigen Wegs gefahren.

## CHIDHER

Chidher, the always young one, spoke:
To a great city I drew near;
A man fruit in his orchard broke.
I asked how long this town was here.
And he, still plucking apples, says:
"This city has been here always,
And will be, to the end of days."
And when five hundred years went by,
Down that same roadway traveled I.

But of the town there was no sign:
A herdsman blew his reed-pipe here
And in the meadow grazed his kine.
"When did the city disappear?"
I asked; he, while he further plays,
Says: "One herb grows, the next decays,
And here my herd will always graze."
And when five hundred years went by,
Down that same roadway traveled I.

A sea now showed its wavy crests;
A boatsman casts his fishnets near,
And while from heavy toil he rests
I ask since when this sea was here.
And, laughing at my words, he says:
"So long the wave the harbor sprays,
The fisher with his fishnets stays."
And when five hundred years went by,
Down that same roadway traveled I.

Da fand ich einen waldigen Raum
Und einen Mann in der Siedelei,
Er fällte mit der Axt den Baum;
Ich fragte, wie alt der Wald hier sei?
Er sprach: „Der Wald ist ein ewiger Hort!
Schon ewig wohn ich an diesem Ort,
Und ewig wachsen die Bäum hier fort." –
Und aber nach fünfhundert Jahren
Kam ich desselbigen Wegs gefahren.

Da fand ich eine Stadt, und laut
Erschallte der Markt vom Volksgeschrei.
Ich fragte: Seit wann ist die Stadt erbaut?
Wohin ist Wald und Meer und Schalmei?
Sie schrien und hörten nicht mein Wort:
„So ging es ewig an diesem Ort
Und wird es gehen ewig fort." –
Und aber nach fünfhundert Jahren
Will ich desselbigen Weges fahren.

But now a forest there I see;
And of a man who tries to clear
A place by cutting down a tree
I ask how long these woods were here.
He says: "They have been here always;
Meseems forever did I gaze
Upon these oaks and pines and bays."
And when five hundred years went by,
Down that same roadway traveled I.

I saw a city that was filled
With clamor of the market day.
I asked: "When was this city built?
Sea, woods and meadows, where are they?"
Not heeding me, they loudly praise
Their city: "It was here always
And will be, till the end of days."
Again this same old road shall I
Tread, when five hundred years go by.

                                    *Martin Zwart*

*August von Platen*

## DAS GRAB IM BUSENTO

Nächtlich am Busento lispeln, bei Cosenza, dumpfe Lieder;
Aus den Wassern schallt es Antwort, und in Wirbeln klingt es wider!

Und den Fluß hinauf, hinunter ziehn die Schatten tapfrer Goten,
Die den Alarich beweinen, ihres Volkes besten Toten.

Allzufrüh und fern der Heimat mußten hier sie ihn begraben,
Während noch die Jugendlocken seine Schulter blond umgaben.

Und am Ufer des Busento reihten sie sich um die Wette,
Um die Strömung abzuleiten, gruben sie ein frisches Bette.

In der wogenleeren Höhlung wühlten sie empor die Erde,
Senkten tief hinein den Leichnam, mit der Rüstung, auf dem Pferde.

Deckten dann mit Erde wieder ihn und seine stolze Habe,
Daß die hohen Stromgewächse wüchsen aus dem Heldengrabe.

Abgelenkt zum zweiten Male, ward der Fluß herbeigezogen:
Mächtig in ihr altes Bette schäumten die Busentowogen.

Und es sang ein Chor von Männern: „Schlaf in deinen Heldenehren!
Keines Römers schnöde Habsucht soll dir je dein Grab versehren!"

Sangen's, und die Lobgesänge tönten fort im Gotenheere;
Wälze sie, Busentowelle, wälze sie von Meer zu Meere!

## THE GRAVE IN THE BUSENTO

Nights one hears on the Busento near Cosenza muffled singing:
Echoes answer from the waters, from the depths seem to be ringing,
Shades of valiant Goths move back and forth in ghostly lamentation,
Mourning the death of Alaric, the greatest leader of their nation,
Whom they sadly had to bury far from home and not much older
Than a youth, when golden hair locks were still flowing 'round his
  shoulder.
The Busento's course to alter, troughs they dug and dams erected,
Hard they worked in hot contention till the current was deflected.
In the old dry river bed then, where a grave they had been digging,
Lowered they their hero's body with his horse and all its rigging;
Him, his arms and proud possessions they with earth again did
  cover,
So tall water-nourished plants above the grave would grow and
  hover.
Then, a second time rechanneled, back came the Busento river;
Mightily the foaming torrent set its regained banks to quiver.
And the warriors sang in chorus: Sleep a hero's peace! for no man
Shall henceforth disturb thy grave, it's sheltered from the greedy
  Roman!
Thus the faithful Gothic soldiers sung their praise and their
  devotion;
Sound it forth, rolling Busento, from thy source unto the ocean!

*Martin Zwart*

## DER PILGRIM VOR ST. JUST

Nacht ists und Stürme sausen für und für,
Hispanische Mönche, schließt mir auf die Tür!

Laßt hier mich ruhn, bis Glockenton mich weckt,
Der zum Gebet euch in die Kirche schreckt!

Bereitet mir, was euer Haus vermag,
Ein Ordenskleid und einen Sarkophag!

Gönnt mir die kleine Zelle, weiht mich ein,
Mehr als die Hälfte dieser Welt war mein.

Das Haupt, das nun der Schere sich bequemt,
Mit mancher Krone ward's bediademt.

Die Schulter, die der Kutte nun sich bückt,
Hat kaiserlicher Hermelin geschmückt.

Nun bin ich vor dem Tod den Toten gleich.
Und fall in Trümmer wie das alte Reich.

THE PILGRIM OF ST. JUST

Pitch-black the night, and loud the tempests roar.
O, Spanish monks, come open me the door.

Here let me rest and let me stay
Till morning bell awakens you to pray.

Prepare for me the raiment that is meet,
A cowl, a mantle and a winding sheet.

Within a narrow cell let me recline.
Once, more than half the world was mine.

The head that many a jewelled crown has worn
Awaits the shears, so let it now be shorn.

To don the cowl this shoulder bends low down
That once has worn a royal ermine gown.

Now before death like a dead man I stand
And fall in ruins like my ancient land.

*Oliver Brown*

*Heinrich Heine*

### DIE WALLFAHRT NACH KEVLAAR

Am Fenster stand die Mutter,
Im Bette lag der Sohn.
„Willst du nicht aufstehn, Wilhelm,
Zu schaun die Prozession?"

„Ich bin so krank, o Mutter,
Daß ich nicht hör' und seh';
Ich denk' an das tote Gretchen,
Da tut das Herz mir weh." –

„Steh' auf, wir wollen nach Kevlaar,
Nimm Buch und Rosenkranz;
Die Mutter-Gottes heilt dir
Dein krankes Herze ganz."

Es flattern die Kirchenfahnen,
Es singt im Kirchenton;
Das ist zu Köln am Rheine,
Da geht die Prozession.

Die Mutter folgt der Menge,
Den Sohn, den führet sie,
Sie singen beide im Chore:
„Gelobt seist du, Marie!"

Die Mutter-Gottes zu Kevlaar
Trägt heut ihr bestes Kleid;
Heut hat sie viel zu schaffen,
Es kommen viel' kranke Leut'.

## THE PILGRIMAGE TO KEVLAAR

The mother stood by the window,
Abed the son did lie.
"Oh, won't you rise, my William,
To see the procession go by?"

"I am so ill, my mother,
Can neither see nor hear;
My heart it aches when recalling
Sweet Margaret on her bier."

"Arise, we shall go to Kevlaar,
Take Book and rosary;
The Saviour's mother relieveth
Your heart from agony."

The holy banners are waving
And singing in unison,
The church procession traverses
The Rhenish town of Cologne.

She joins the thronging pilgrims,
And leads him tenderly,
They both intone the chorus:
"Maria, praise to Thee!"

Today the Virgin of Kevlaar
Is decked in her finest array:
So many sick are coming,
She has much work today.

Die kranken Leute bringen
Ihr dar als Opferspend'
Aus Wachs gebildete Glieder,
Viel wächserne Füß' und Händ'.

Und wer eine Wachshand opfert,
Dem heilt an der Hand die Wund';
Und wer einen Wachsfuß opfert,
Dem wird der Fuß gesund.

Nach Kevlaar ging mancher auf Krücken,
Der jetzo tanzt auf dem Seil.
Gar mancher spielt jetzt die Bratsche,
Dem dort kein Finger war heil.

Die Mutter nahm ein Wachslicht,
Und bildete draus ein Herz.
,,Bring das der Mutter-Gottes,
Dann heilt sie deinen Schmerz.''

Der Sohn nahm seufzend das Wachsherz,
Ging seufzend zum Heiligenbild;
Die Träne quillt aus dem Auge,
Das Wort aus dem Herzen quillt:

,,Du hochgebenedeite,
Du reine Gottesmagd,
Du Königin des Himmels,
Dir sei mein Leid geklagt!

Ich wohnte mit meiner Mutter,
Zu Köllen in der Stadt,
Der Stadt, die viele hundert
Kapellen und Kirchen hat.

For offering, the crippled
Are bringing to her seat,
Some moulded, waxen members,
And waxen hands and feet.

The wounds on the hand that offers
A waxen hand will close;
And he, who offers a wax foot,
Gets well from heel to toes.

To Kevlaar came many on crutches,
Who dance anon on a rope,
Fair many play the viol,
Whose every finger was broke.

The mother took a taper,
And shaped therefrom a heart
"Take this to Jesus' mother,
Then She will heal your smart."

The son took sighing the wax heart;
He went to the shrine and demurred;
The tear from the eye was flowing,
And from the heart the word.

"Thou pure and blessed Virgin,
Thou maiden of the Lord.
Thou Queen of all the Heaven,
May'st Thou my plaint record.

I lived in Cologne with my mother,
The city afar renowned,
For many are its churches
And chapels in it abound.

Und neben uns wohnte Gretchen,
Doch die ist tot jetzund –
Marie, dir bring ich ein Wachsherz,
Heil' du meine Herzenswund'.

Heil' du mein krankes Herze–
Ich will auch spät und früh
Inbrünstiglich beten und singen:
Gelobt seist du, Marie!"

Der kranke Sohn und die Mutter,
Sie schliefen im Kämmerlein;
Da kam die Mutter-Gottes
Ganz leise geschritten herein.

Sie beugte sich über den Kranken,
Und legte ihre Hand
Ganz leise auf sein Herze,
Und lächelte mild und schwand.

Die Mutter schaut alles im Traume,
Und hat noch mehr geschaut;
Sie erwachte aus dem Schlummer,
Die Hunde bellten so laut.

Da lag dahingestrecket
Ihr Sohn, und der war tot;
Es spielt auf den bleichen Wangen
Das lichte Morgenrot.

Die Mutter faltet' die Hände,
Ihr war, sie wußte nicht wie;
Andächtig sang sie leise:
,,Gelobt seist du, Marie!"

And Margaret lived near us,
But she is dead and gone—
Maria, I bring Thee a wax heart,
Heal Thou my heart anon.

Heal Thou my heart that is aching,
And I will fervently
For ever chant thy prayer:
"Maria, praise to Thee!"

The ailing son and his mother,
Were lying asleep on their bed,
When Mary, the mother of Jesus,
Came in with silent tread.

And over the sufferer bending,
She laid her hand for a while
Upon his heart, oh so gently,
And vanished with a smile.

The mother, who still was sleeping,
Saw all in her dream and more.
She wakened from her slumber,
Loud howled the dogs by the door.

And there, stretched out, was lying
Her son, in death withdrawn.
Upon his waxen features,
The rosy light of dawn.

The mother, she folded in prayer,
Her hands, so strange felt she;
And sang, devoutly, softly,
"Maria, praise to Thee!"

*Helen Kurz Roberts*

BELSAZER

Die Mitternacht zog näher schon;
In stummer Ruh lag Babylon.

Nur oben in des Königs Schloß,
Da flackerts, da lärmt des Königs Troß.

Dort oben in dem Königssaal
Belsazer hielt sein Königsmahl.

Die Knechte saßen in schimmernden Reihn
Und leerten die Becher mit funkelndem Wein.

Es klirrten die Becher, es jauchzten die Knecht;
So klang es dem störrigen Könige recht.

Des Königs Wangen leuchten Glut;
Im Wein erwuchs ihm kecker Mut.

Und blindlings reißt der Mut ihn fort;
Und er lästert die Gottheit mit sündigem Wort.

Und er brüstet sich frech und lästert wild!
Die Knechteschar ihm Beifall brüllt.

Der König rief mit stolzem Blick;
Der Diener eilt und kehrt zurück.

Er trug viel gülden Gerät auf dem Haupt,
Das war aus dem Tempel Jehovas geraubt.

BELSHAZZAR

The midnight hour was coming on
In quiet repose lay Babylon.

But the king's palace on the height
Was full of noise and flickering light.

High up there in the royal halls
The king was feasting with his thralls.

The glittering warriors line by line
Were draining cups of sparkling wine.

There was shouting of men and the beakers did ring;
How that pleased the ear of the stubborn king.

His cheeks from toping were aglow
And each cup made his courage grow.

And drunk he curses suddenly
With sinful words the deity.

And with insolent boasts he blasphemes and raves
To the bellowing cheers of warriors and slaves.

A haughty glance – a servant runs
And to the king returns at once.

And on his head the vessels sway
From Jehovah's temple in golden array.

Und der König ergriff mit frevler Hand
Einen heiligen Becher, gefüllt bis am Rand.

Und er leert ihn hastig bis auf den Grund
Und rufet laut mit schäumendem Mund:

„Jehova! dir künd ich auf ewig Hohn –
Ich bin der König von Babylon!"

Doch kaum das grause Wort verklang,
Dem König wards heimlich im Busen bang.

Das gellende Lachen verstummte zumal;
Es wurde leichenstill im Saal.

Und sieh! und sieh! an weißer Wand,
Da kams hervor, wie Menschenhand;

Und schrieb, und schrieb an weißer Wand
Buchstaben von Feuer, und schrieb und schwand.

Der König stieren Blicks da saß,
Mit schlotternden Knien und totenblaß.

Die Knechteschar saß kalt durchgraut
Und saß gar still, gab keinen Laut.

Die Magier kamen, doch keiner verstand
Zu deuten die Flammenschrift an der Wand.

Belsazer ward aber in selbiger Nacht
Von seinen Knechten umgebracht.

And the royal blasphemer seized and spilled
A sacred beaker quickly filled

And emptied it quickly to the dregs
And with foaming lips he shouts and brags:

"I mock thee, Jehovah; thou art undone,
I am the Great King of Babylon!"

The gruesome word was scarcely said,
The king's heart felt a secret dread.

There was no brazen laughter then
Silent like corpses sat the men.

And see, see there! near the white wall's end
Something came forth like a human hand

And wrote, and wrote near the white wall's end
Letters of fire, and wrote and went.

Pale as a corpse the king sat there
With shaking knees and a dead man's stare.

The king's own guard sat horror-bound
Chilled to the heart and made no sound.

The wise men came but none of all
Could read the flame script on the wall.

But in his palace this same night
By the sword of his men Belshazzar died.

*Meno Spann*

*August Kopisch*

### DER NÖCK

Es tönt des Nöcken Harfenschall:
Da steht der wilde Wasserfall,
Unschwebt mit Schaum und Wogen
Den Nöck im Regenbogen;
Die Bäume neigen
Sich tief und schweigen,
Und atmend horcht die Nachtigall. –

„O Nöck, was hilft das Singen dein?
Du kannst ja doch nicht selig sein!
Wie kann dein Singen taugen?" –
Der Nöck erhebt die Augen,
Sieht an die Kleinen,
Beginnt zu weinen . . .
Und senkt sich in die Flut hinein.

Da rauscht und braust der Wasserfall,
Hoch fliegt hinweg die Nachtigall;
Die Bäume heben mächtig
Die Häupter grün und prächtig!
O weh, es haben
Die wilden Knaben
Den Nöck betrübt im Wasserfall!

„Komm wieder. Nöck, du singst so schön!
Wer singt. kann in den Himmel gehn!
Du wirst mit deinem Klingen
Zum Paradiese dringen!

## THE NIX

The nix, he plays his harp: in thrall,
Suspended hangs the waterfall,
With foam and waves that hover,
It builds a rainbow cover.
The trees are bending,
In silence attending,
And breathing lists the nightingale.

"O Nix, your song is sung in vain,
Eternal bliss you cannot gain,
Why do you sing? I wonder."
The nix looks up and yonder.
He sighs on spying
The boys, and crying
He sinks deep down into the flood.

The waterfall, now rushing, roars,
The nightingale to heaven soars,
The mighty trees, unbended,
Raise verdant crowns and splendid.
The spell is ended,
The boys offended
The nix who dwells beneath the fall.

"O Nix, we like your singing best!
Come back, who sings may yet be bless't,
And, with your harp still ringing,
You'll join the angels singing.

O komm, es haben
Gescherzt die Knaben:
Komm wieder, Nöck, und singe schön!"

Da tönt des Nöckes Harfenschall,
Und wieder steht der Wasserfall,
Umschwebt mit Schaum und Wogen
Den Nöck im Regenbogen,
Die Bäume neigen
Sich tief und schweigen
Und atmend horcht die Nachtigall.

Es spielt der Nöck und singt mit Macht
Von Meer und Erd' und Himmelspracht.
Mit Singen kann er lachen
Und selig weinen machen! –
Der Wald erbebet,
Die Sonn' entschwebet . . .
Er singt bis in die Sternennacht.

The jest is ended,
The boys pretended,
Return, O Nix, and sing again!"

The nix, he plays once more; in thrall,
Again suspended hangs the fall,
With foam and waves that hover,
It builds a rainbow cover.
The trees are bending,
In silence attending,
And breathing lists the nightingale.

The nix, he plays and sings with might,
Of sea and earth, the heavens bright.
His singing can bring laughter,
And blissful tears thereafter.
The woods are swaying,
The sky is graying,
He sings into the starlit night.

*Helen Kurz Roberts*

*Nikolaus Lenau*

### DER POSTILLION

Lieblich war die Maiennacht,
Silberwölklein flogen,
Ob der holden Frühlingspracht
Freudig hingezogen.

Schlummernd lagen Wies' und Hain,
Jeder Pfad verlassen;
Niemand als der Mondenschein
Wachte auf den Straßen.

Leise nur das Lüftchen sprach,
Und es zog gelinder
Durch das stille Schlafgemach
All der Frühlingskinder.

Heimlich nur das Bächlein schlich;
Denn der Blüten Träume
Dufteten gar wonniglich
Durch die stillen Räume.

Rauher war mein Postillion
Ließ die Geißel knallen,
Über Berg und Tal davon
Frisch sein Horn erschallen.

Und von flinken Rossen vier
Scholl der Hufe Schlagen,
Die durchs blühende Revier
Trabten mit Behagen.

## THE POSTILLION

Lovely was that night in May,
Silver clouds were sailing
High above fair spring's display
Gaily thither trailing.

Silent lay the field, the wood,
Lonely every byway;
No one but the moon who stood
Watching o'er the highway.

But in whispers spoke the air,
Wafting, scent-encumbered,
Through the silent chambers, where
All spring's children slumbered.

But in secret crept the brook,
For the dreams of flowers
Filled with fragrance every nook
In those silent hours.

My postillion was less still,
Cracked his whip, unfounded,
Over valley over hill
Clear his post horn sounded.

And four horses' nimble feet
Struck the ground in measure,
As they trotted through the beat,
All in bloom, with pleasure.

Wald und Flur im schnellen Zug
Kaum gegrüßt – gemieden;
Und vorbei, wie Traumesflug,
Schwand der Dörfer Frieden.

Mitten in dem Maienglück
Lag ein Kirchhof innen,
Der den raschen Wanderblick
Hielt zu ernstem Sinnen.

Hingelehnt an Bergesrand
War die bleiche Mauer,
Und das Kreuzbild Gottes stand
Hoch, in stummer Trauer.

Schwager ritt auf seiner Bahn
Stiller jetzt und trüber;
Und die Rosse hielt er an,
Sah zum Kreuz hinüber:

„Halten muß hier Roß und Rad!
Mag's Euch nicht gefährden;
Drüben liegt mein Kamerad
In der kühlen Erden!

Ein gar herzlieber Gesell!
Herr, 's ist ewig schade!
Keiner blies das Horn so hell
Wie mein Kamerade!

Hier ich immer halten muß,
Dem dort unterm Rasen
Zum getreuen Brudergruß
Sein Leiblied zu blasen!"

Lea and copse appeared and fled
Mocking in derision,
And the peaceful hamlets sped
Past, like flights of vision.

Right amidst this vernal bliss
Lay a churchyard winking,
Made the joy seem quite amiss,
Set the mind athinking.

Leaning on the mountainside
Was the pale enclosure
And above the Crucified
Rose in sad composure.

My postillion's merry ways
Changed, he seemed to ponder;
Then he stopped and turned his gaze
To the cross up yonder.

"Horse and wheel must here stand still,
Yet it means no danger,
Over there in graveyard chill
Lies a fellow ranger.

Sir, he was my friend and dear,
'Tis the greatest pity!
None could blow the horn so clear
None so nice a ditty!

'Tis for him I call this rest,
Him I shall be treating
To the tunes he once liked best
As a friendly greeting.

Und dem Kirchhof sandt er zu
Frohe Wandersänge,
Daß es in die Grabesruh
Seinem Bruder dränge.

Und des Hornes heller Ton
Klang vom Berge wieder,
Ob der tote Postillion
Stimmt' in seine Lieder. –

Weiter ging's durch Feld und Hag
Mit verhängtem Zügel;
Lang mir noch im Ohre lag
Jener Klang vom Hügel.

To the graveyard he did send
Merry songs aswelling,
So that they might reach his friend
In his silent dwelling.

And the post horn's silver-tone
From the hill rebounded,
Just as though beneath the stone
T'other horn had sounded.

On we sped and past the mounds,
Skirting hedges, meadows;
Long my ear retained those sounds
From the hill of shadows.

*Helen Kurz Roberts*

## DIE DREI

Drei Reiter nach verlorner Schlacht,
Wie reiten sie so sacht, so sacht!

Aus tiefen Wunden quillt das Blut,
Es spürt das Roß die warme Flut.

Vom Sattel tropft das Blut, vom Zaum,
Und spült hinunter Staub und Schaum.

Die Rosse schreiten sanft und weich,
Sonst flöss' das Blut zu rasch, zu reich.

Die Reiter reiten dicht gesellt,
Und einer sich am andern hält.

Sie sehn sich traurig ins Gesicht,
Und einer um den andern spricht:

„Mir blüht daheim die schönste Maid,
Drum tut mein früher Tod mir leid."

„Hab' Haus und Hof und grünen Wald,
Und sterben muß ich hier so bald!"

„Den Blick hab' ich in Gottes Welt,
Sonst nichts, doch schwer mir's Sterben fällt."

Und lauernd auf den Todesritt
Ziehn durch die Luft drei Geier mit.

Sie teilen kreischend unter sich:
„Den speisest du, den du, den ich."

## THE THREE

Three riders after harsh defeat,
How slowly, slowly they retreat!

From deep-cut gashes flows their blood,
The horses feel the tepid flood.

From saddle drips the blood, from rein,
And washes dust off flank and mane.

The steed's advance is gently slow,
Or else too swift the blood's rich flow.

The dying horsemen, side by side,
Clasp one another while they ride,

And each with mien disconsolate
Now mourns that this should be his fate:

"A maid has promised me her hand —
Why must I die in foreign land?"

"Have home and farm and forest green,
And meet a death so unforeseen!"

"God gave me life, his only boon,
And yet I dread to die so soon."

And where they on their death-ride fare,
Three vultures follow through the air.

They share the men with piercing cry:
"Him you devour, him you, him I!"

*Gerd Gillhoff*

*Eduard Möricke*

### SCHÖN-ROHTRAUT

Wie heißt König Ringangs Töchterlein?
Rohtraut, Schön-Rohtraut.
Was tut sie denn den ganzen Tag,
Da sie wohl nicht spinnen und nähen mag?
Tut fischen und jagen.
O daß ich doch ihr Jäger wär!
Fischen und Jagen freute mich sehr.
– Schweig stille, mein Herze!

Und über eine kleine Weil,
Rohtraut, Schön-Rohtraut,
So dient der Knab auf Ringangs Schloß
In Jägertracht und hat ein Roß,
Mit Rohtraut zu jagen.
O daß ich doch ein Königssohn wär!
Rohtraut, Schön-Rohtraut lieb ich so sehr.
– Schweig stille, mein Herze!

Einsmals sie ruhten am Eichenbaum,
Da lacht Schön-Rohtraut:
,,Was siehst mich an so wunniglich?
Wenn du das Herz hast, küsse mich!"
Ach! erschrak der Knabe!
Doch denket er: ,,Mir ist's vergunnt",
Und küsset Schön-Rohtraut auf den Mund.
– Schweig stille, mein Herze!

Darauf sie ritten schweigend heim,
Rohtraut, Schön-Rohtraut;
Es jauchzt der Knab in seinem Sinn!

## FAIR ROHTRAUT

Oh, what is the name of King Ringang's daughter?
Rohtraut, Fair Rohtraut.
And what does she do the live-long day,
Since she scarcely would spin and knit alway?
She goes fishing and hunting.
Oh, that her huntsman I might be!
I'd fish and hunt right merrily.
– Ah, be silent, my heart!

And after just a little while,
Rohtraut, Fair Rohtraut,
The lad did serve at Ringang's court
In squire's garb and had a horse,
To hunt with Rohtraut.
Oh, that a king's son I might be!
I love Fair Rohtraut tenderly.
– Ah, be silent, my heart!

One day they stopped by an old oak tree,
Then laughed Fair Rohtraut:
"Why look at me so blissfully?
If you have courage, come, kiss me!"
Oh, how startled the lad was!
And yet he thinks: 'Twas offered me,"
And kisses Fair Rohtraut tenderly.
– Ah, be silent, my heart!

And then they rode quite silent home,
Rohtraut, Fair Rohtraut;
The lad exulted all the way:

„Und würdest du heute Kaiserin,
Mich sollt's nicht kränken !
Ihr tausend Blätter im Walde wißt,
Ich hab Schön-Rohtrauts Mund geküßt !
– Schweig stille, mein Herze!"

Though you were made an Empress today,
It would not grieve me;
Ye thousand leaves in the forest, hear!
I've kissed Fair Rohtraut's mouth so dear!
Ah, be silent, my heart!

*Isabel S. MacInnes*

*Gottfried Keller*

DIE ÖFFENTLICHEN VERLEUMDER

Ein Ungeziefer ruht
In Staub und trocknem Schlamme
Verborgen, wie die Flamme
In leichter Asche tut.
Ein Regen, Windeshauch
Erweckt das schlimme Leben,
Und aus dem Nichts erheben
Sich Seuchen, Glut und Rauch.

Aus dunkler Höhle fährt
Ein Schächer, um zu schweifen;
Nach Beuteln möcht' er greifen
Und findet bessern Wert:
Er findet einen Streit
Um nichts, ein irres Wissen,
Ein Banner, das zerrissen,
Ein Volk in Blödigkeit.

Er findet, wo er geht,
Die Leere dürft'ger Zeiten,
Da kann er schamlos schreiten,
Nun wird er ein Prophet;
Auf einen Kehricht stellt
Er seine Schelmenfüße
Und zischelt seine Grüße
In die verblüffte Welt.

Gehüllt in Niedertracht
Gleichwie in einer Wolke,

## THE CHARACTER ASSASSINS

A breed of vermin lies
In dust and dry rot hidden,
As flame oft glows unbidden
In ashes and not dies.
Comes playful wind or rain
And wakes this baleful scourge,
From chaos swift emerge
Foul plague and fire and pain.

On booty bent 'there came
From his nocturnal cave
A pocket-picking knave.
But he finds better game:
He finds a flag torn down,
The facts of knowledge muddled,
A people all befuddled
By discord's petty frown.

On all sides he finds slums,
Depression's aimlessness,
And now in shamelessness
A prophet he becomes;
His blessings are unfurled,
As he bestrides destruction
To hiss his foul instruction
To the bedeviled world.

All clothed in scoundrelcy
As in a turgid cloud,

Ein Lügner vor dem Volke,
Ragt bald er groß an Macht
Mit seiner Helfer Zahl,
Die, hoch und niedrig stehend,
Gelegenheit erspähend,
Sich bieten seiner Wahl.

Sie teilen aus sein Wort,
Wie einst die Gottesboten
Getan mit den fünf Broten,
Das klecket fort und fort!
Erst log allein der Hund,
Nun lügen ihrer tausend;
Und wie ein Sturm erbrausend,
So wuchert jetzt sein Pfund.

Hoch schießt empor die Saat,
Verwandelt sind die Lande,
Die Menge lebt in Schande
Und lacht der Schofeltat!
Jetzt hat sich auch erwahrt,
Was erstlich war erfunden:
Die Guten sind verschwunden,
Die Schlechten stehn geschart!

Wenn einstmals diese Not
Lang wie ein Eis gebrochen,
Dann wird davon gesprochen,
Wie von dem schwarzen Tod;
Und einen Strohmann baun
Die Kinder auf der Heide,
Zu brennen Lust aus Leide
Und Licht aus altem Graun.

A public liar loud,
A mighty pow'r is he
With helpers manifold
In high and lowly station,
Each seeking elevation,
And each to his will sold.

His gospel word they spread,
It multiplies apace,
As once God's men of grace
Dealt out five loaves of bread.
The dog first lies alone,
Then thousands tell his lies;
His dim wit magnifies
Into a storm full blown.

A mighty harvest breeds,
The lands are ne'er the same,
The masses live in shame
And laugh at knavish deeds!
And now it has come true,
The warning no one feared:
The good have disappeared,
The bad are in full view.

When someday hence this ague
Like ice at length is broken,
We'll speak of it in token
As of bubonic plague.
And children will of straw
Make effigies on the plain,
New joy to burn from pain
And light from ancient awe.

*Harold Lenz*

*Theodor Fontane*

## ARCHIBALD DOUGLAS

„Ich hab es getragen sieben Jahr,
Und ich kann es tragen nicht mehr,
Wo immer die Welt am schönsten war,
Da war sie öd und leer.

Ich will hintreten vor sein Gesicht
In dieser Knechtsgestalt,
Er kann meine Bitte versagen nicht,
Ich bin ja worden alt.

Und trüg er noch den alten Groll,
Frisch wie am ersten Tag,
So komme, was da kommen soll,
Und komme, was da mag."

Graf Douglas sprichts. Am Weg ein Stein
Lud ihn zu harter Ruh,
Er sah in Wald und Feld hinein,
Die Augen fielen ihm zu.

Er trug einen Harnisch, rostig und schwer,
Darüber ein Pilgerkleid –
Da horch, vom Waldrand scholl es her
Wie von Hörnern und Jagdgeleit.

Und Kies und Staub aufwirbelte dicht,
Herjagte Meut und Mann,
Und ehe der Graf sich aufgericht't,
Waren Roß und Reiter heran.

## ARCHIBALD DOUGLAS

"The life I have borne for seven years,
I can no longer bear,
Wherever the world most fair appears,
Tis bleak and empty there.

"To face him as I am is best,
A menial to behold,
He cannot in fairness refuse my request,
For I have grown so old.

"And should his grudge and his distrust
Be fresh as they were the first day,
Then happen will, what happen must,
Let happen whatever may."

Thus spoke Lord Douglas. A stone by the way
Invited to hard repose,
He looked out to where field and forest lay,
And his eyes began to close.

His heavy, rusty mail was worn,
Beneath a pilgrim's gown –
But hark! from the wood the sound of the horn
And of huntsmen came floating down.

And chasing along came man and hound
That gravel and dust rose high,
And ere the lord got up from the ground,
The horse and its rider were nigh.

König Jakob saß auf hohem Roß,
Graf Douglas grüßte tief;
Dem König das Blut in die Wange schoß,
Der Douglas aber rief:

,,König Jakob, schaue mich gnädig an
Und höre mich in Geduld!
Was meine Brüder dir angetan,
Es war nicht meine Schuld.

Denk nicht an den alten Douglas-Neid,
Der trotzig dich bekriegt,
Denk lieber an deine Kinderzeit,
Wo ich dich auf den Knien gewiegt.

Denk lieber zurück an Stirling-Schloß,
Wo ich Spielzeug dir geschnitzt,
Dich gehoben auf deines Vaters Roß
Und Pfeile dir zugespitzt.

Denk lieber zurück an Linlithgow,
An den See und den Vogelherd,
Wo ich dich fischen und jagen froh
Und schwimmen und springen gelehrt.

O, denk an alles, was einsten war,
Und sänftige deinen Sinn —
Ich hab es gebüßet sieben Jahr,
Daß ich ein Douglas bin.''

,,Ich seh dich nicht, Graf Archibald,
Ich hör deine Stimme nicht;
Mir ist, als ob ein Rauschen im Wald
Von alten Zeiten spricht.

King James, on his stallion proud, stopped dead.
Lord Douglas humbly bowed;
A blush the King's cheeks overspread,
But the Douglas called out aloud:

"King James, oh look on me graciously,
With patience thine ear incline!
Whatever my brothers have done to thee,
The fault has not been mine.

"Forget the Douglas' jealous ways,
That they fought thee stubbornly,
But rather remember thy childhood days,
When I rocked thee on my knee.

"Recall the Castle of Stirling so fair,
Where I carved for thee many a toy,
Where I lifted thee up on thy father's mare,
And sharpened thy darts when a boy.

"The memories of Linlithgow revive,
Of its lake and its fowling place,
Where I taught thee how to swim and dive,
How to fish and to follow the chase.

"Oh, think of all that once has been,
Let soften thy heart and relent,
By seven weary years and lean,
I atoned for my Douglas descent."

"I do not see thee, Lord Archibald,
I do not hear thy voice,
But a rustling in the wood recalled
The times when I could rejoice.

Mir klingt das Rauschen süß und traut,
Ich lausch ihm immer noch;
Dazwischen aber klingt es laut:
Er ist ein Douglas doch!

Ich seh dich nicht, ich höre dich nicht,
Das ist alles, was ich kann;
Ein Douglas vor meinem Angesicht
Wär ein verlorener Mann."

König Jakob gab seinem Roß den Sporn;
Bergan ging jetzt sein Ritt,
Graf Douglas faßte den Zügel vorn
Und hielt mit dem Könige Schritt.

Der Weg war steil, und die Sonne stach,
Und sein Panzerhemd war schwer;
Doch ob er schier zusammenbrach,
Er lief doch nebenher.

,,König Jakob, ich war dein Seneschall,
Ich will es nicht fürder sein,
Ich will nur warten dein Roß im Stall
Und ihm schütten die Körner ein;

Ich will ihm selber machen die Streu
Und es tränken mit eigener Hand:
Nur laß mich atmen wieder aufs neu
Die Luft im Vaterland!

Und willst du nicht, so hab einen Mut,
Und ich will es danken dir,
Und zieh dein Schwert und triff mich gut
Und laß mich sterben hier!"

"A rustling, sweetly familiar,
I listen to it yet,
But in between a dissonant bar,
A Douglas he is! don't forget!

"I see thee not, I hear thee not,
That is all I can do for thee.
A Douglas, stood he in this spot,
A man undone would be."

King James thereon set spurs to his horse,
The ride went uphill to the crest,
Lord Douglas gripped the reins with force,
And kept with the king abreast.

The way was steep and hot the day,
And heavily weighed the mail,
Yet though his strength gave almost way,
He ran by the side of the trail.

"To be Master of the Horse again,
My King, I have no call,
But let me pour for thy mount the grain,
And groom him in his stall.

"His litter I myself shall strew,
And his bucket to him I shall hand,
But only let me breathe anew
The air in my fatherland.

"Yet wilt thou not, then pity discard,
I shall deem it an act of grace,
And draw thy sword and hit me hard
And let me die in this place."

König Jakob sprang herab vom Pferd,
Hell leuchtete sein Gesicht;
AusderScheidezog ersein breitesSchwert,
Aber fallen ließ er es nicht.

„Nimms hin, nimms hin und trag es neu
Und bewache mir meine Ruh!
Der ist in tiefster Seele treu,
Der die Heimat liebt wie du.

Zu Roß! wir reiten nach Linlithgow,
Und du reitest an meiner Seit;
Da wollen wir fischen und jagen froh
Als wie in alter Zeit."

King James he vaulted down from his steed,
His face with joy aglow,
His broadsword he unsheathed indeed,
But he never struck the blow.

"Oh take it, take it into thy trust,
And guard my slumbers anew!
Who loves his homeland the way thou dost,
In his deepest soul he is true.

"On horseback I go to Linlithgow with thee,
Thou ridest beside me, nigh,
And there we shall fish and hunt with glee
As we did in days gone by."

                                        *Helen Kurz Roberts*

## DIE BRÜCKE AM TAY

### 28. Dezember 1879

When shall we three meet again? (Macbeth)


„Wann treffen wir drei wieder zusamm?"
„Um die siebente Stund, am Brückendamm."
„Am Mittelpfeiler."
            „Ich lösche die Flamm."
„Ich mit."
       „Ich komme vom Norden her."
„Und ich vom Süden."
             „Und ich vom Meer."
„Hei, das gibt einen Ringelreihn,
Und die Brücke muß in den Grund hinein."
„Und der Zug, der in die Brücke tritt
Um die siebente Stund?"
           „Ei, der muß mit."
„Muß mit."
    „Tand, Tand
Ist das Gebilde von Menschenhand!"


Auf der Norderseite das Brückenhaus –
Alle Fenster sehen nach Süden aus,
Und die Brücknersleut ohne Rast und Ruh
Und in Bangen sehen nach Süden zu,
Sehen und warten, ob nicht ein Licht
Übers Wasser hin „Ich komme" spricht,
„Ich komme, trotz Nacht und Sturmesflug,
Ich, der Edinburger Zug."


Und der Brückner jetzt: „Ich seh einen Schein
Am anderen Ufer. Das muß er sein.
Nun, Mutter, weg mit dem bangen Traum,

## THE BRIDGE ON THE TAY

### (December 28, 1879)

When shall we three meet again? (Macbeth)


"When shall we three meet again?"
"By the bridge, at seven, down the lane."
"By the middle pier."

                    "I put out the flame."
"I too."

          "I come from the northern sphere."
"And I from the south."

                         "From the sea I come here."
"A merry dance it will be, ho! ho!
And down to the bottom the bridge must go."
"And the train that at seven passes through
To cross the bridge?"

                    "Hey, that goes too."
"Goes too."

          "On sand, on sand,
Rests all that is built by human hand."


The bridgekeeper's house on the bank to the north –
All windows to the south look forth,
The keeper, his wife, both restlessly peer,
Towards the south with growing fear,
They watch and wait for a light to say
"Look out, I am coming" across the bay,
"In spite of the night and the hurricane,
Here I come, the Edinburgh train."


And the keeper anon: "That light shows plain
On the other shore. It must be the train.
Now, mother, have done with your nightmares, you see,

Unser Johnie kommt und will seinen Baum,
Und was noch am Baume von Lichtern ist,
Zünd alles an wie zum heiligen Christ,
Der will heuer zweimal mit uns sein –
Und in elf Minuten ist er herein."

Und es war der Zug. Am Süderturm
Keucht er vorbei jetzt gegen den Sturm,
Und Johnie spricht: ,,Die Brücke noch!
Aber was tut es, wir zwingen es doch.
Ein fester Kessel, ein doppelter Dampf,
Die bleiben Sieger in solchem Kampf.
Und wies auch rast und ringt und rennt,
Wir kriegen es unter, das Element.

Und unser Stolz ist unsre Brück;
Ich lache, denk' ich an früher zurück,
An all den Jammer und all die Not
Mit dem elend alten Schifferboot;
Wie manche liebe Christfestnacht
Hab ich im Fährhaus zugebracht
Und sah unsrer Fenster lichten Schein
Und zählte und konnte nicht drüben sein."

Auf der Norderseite, das Brückenhaus –
Alle Fenster sehen nach Süden aus,
Und die Brücknersleut ohne Rast und Ruh
Und in Bangen sehen nach Süden zu;
Denn wütender wurde der Winde Spiel,
Und jetzt, als ob Feuer vom Himmel fiel,
Erglüht es in niederschießender Pracht
Überm Wasser unten . . . Und wieder ist Nacht.

,,Wann treffen wir drei wieder zusamm?"
,,Um Mitternacht, am Bergeskamm."

Our Johnnie is coming and wants his tree.
What candles are left on the tree, you shall light,
So that all will be as on Christmas Night.
We'll celebrate it twice this year –
In eleven minutes it will be here."

And it was the train. It is panting past
The southern tower and into the blast.
And Johnnie is saying: "The bridge comes yet,
But no matter the challenge, it will be met;
A sturdy boiler and double the steam,
And they will be the winning team.
Though on raging and wrestling and rushing bent,
We yet get it under, the element.

"Our bridge it is our pride indeed;
I laugh whenever I think of the need,
Of all the misery and the cold
In that ferryboat, so wretchedly old;
How many a cherished Christmas Night
I spent in the ferryhouse, within sight
Of our windows, that shone with festive glare,
And counted them, and could not be there."

The bridgekeeper's house on the bank to the north –
All windows to the south look forth,
And the keeper, his wife, both restlessly peer
Towards the south with growing fear;
From playful, the winds had been getting high,
And now, as though fires poured forth from the sky,
In downshooting splendor all is alight
On the waters below . . . and again it is night.

"When shall we three meet again?"
"At twelve, on the ridge above the plain."

„Auf dem hohen Moor, am Erlenstamm."
„Ich komme."
   „Ich mit."
      „Ich nenn euch die Zahl."
„Und ich die Namen."
     „Und ich die Qual."
„Hei!
  Wie Splitter brach das Gebälk entzwei."
    „Tand, Tand
Ist das Gebilde von Menschenhand."

"On the Highland moor, by the alders the twain."
"I come."
      "I too."
           "The count I supply."
"And I the names."
              "Their agonies I."
"Hey!
Like chips the girders broke away!"
                "On sand, on sand,
Rests all that is built by human hand."

*Helen Kurz Roberts*

## HERR VON RIBBECK AUF RIBBECK IM HAVELLAND

Herr von Ribbeck auf Ribbeck im Havelland,
Ein Birnbaum in seinem Garten stand,
Und kam die goldene Herbsteszeit
Und die Birnen leuchteten weit und breit,
Da stopfte, wenns Mittag vom Turme scholl,
Der von Ribbeck sich beide Taschen voll,
Und kam in Pantinen ein Junge daher,
So rief er: „Junge, wiste ne Beer?"
Und kam ein Mädel, so rief er: „Lütt Dirn,
Kumm man röwer, ick hebb ne Birn."

So ging es viel Jahre, bis lobesam
Der von Ribbeck auf Ribbeck zu sterben kam.
Er fühlte sein Ende, 's war Herbsteszeit,
Wieder lachten die Birnen weit und breit;
Da sagte von Ribbeck: „Ich scheide nun ab.
Legt mir eine Birne mit ins Grab!"
Und drei Tage drauf, aus dem Doppeldachhaus,
Trugen von Ribbeck sie hinaus.
Alle Bauern und Büdner mit Feiergesicht
Sangen „Jesus meine Zuversicht!"
Und die Kinder klagten, das Herze schwer:
„He ist dod nu. Wer giwt uns nu ne Beer?"

So klagten die Kinder. Das war nicht recht –
Ach, sie kannten den alten Ribbeck schlecht!
Der neue freilich, der knausert und spart,
Hält Park und Birnbaum strenge verwahrt.
Aber der alte, vorahnend schon
Und voll Mißtraun gegen den eigenen Sohn,
Der wußte genau, was damals er tat,

## SQUIRE RIBBECK AT RIBBECK IN HAVELLAND

Squire Ribbeck at Ribbeck in Havelland,
In his garden there stood a pear tree grand,
And when autumn came round, the golden tide,
And pears were glowing far and wide,
Squire Ribbeck, when noon rang out, would first
Fill both his pockets full to burst
And then, when a boy in his clogs came there,
He called: "My lad, do you want a pear?"
He would hail a girl that chanced to pass:
"Come over, I have a pear, little lass!"

Many years thus went, till the noble and high
Squire Ribbeck at Ribbeck came to die.
He felt his end. It was autumntide.
Again pears were smiling far and wide.
"I depart now this life," Squire Ribbeck said,
"I wish that a pear in my grave be laid."
And after three days, from the mansard-roofed hall,
Squire Ribbeck was carried out, 'neath a pall.
All farmers and cottagers, solemn-faced,
Sang: "Jesus, in Thee my trust is placed,"
And the children lamented, with hearts like lead:
"Who'll give us a pear, now that he is dead?"

So the children lamented. It was unkind,
As they did not know old Ribbeck's mind.
True, the new one is skimping niggardly,
Keeps park and pear tree 'neath lock and key;
But having forebodings, the older one,
And full of distrust for his proper son,
Knew well what he did, when the order he gave,

Als um eine Birn ins Grab er bat;
Und im dritten Jahr aus dem stillen Haus
Ein Birnbaumsprößling sproßt heraus.

Und die Jahre gehen wohl auf und ab,
Längst wölbt sich ein Birnbaum über dem Grab,
Und in der goldenen Herbsteszeit
Leuchtets wieder weit und breit,
Und kommt ein Jung übern Kirchhof her,
So flüsterts im Baume: ,,Wiste ne Beer?"
Und kommt ein Mädel, so flüsterts: ,,Lütt Dirn,
Kumm man röwer, ick gew di ne Birn!"

So spendet Segen noch immer die Hand
Des von Ribbeck auf Ribbeck im Havelland.

That a pear should be laid with him in his grave.
From the silent dwelling, after three years,
The tip of a pear tree seedling appears.

And year after year, the seasons go round,
Long since a pear tree is shading the mound.
And in the golden autumntide
Again it is glowing far and wide.
When a boy is crossing the churchyard there,
The tree is whispering: "Want a pear?"
And when a girl chances to pass
It whispers: "Come here for a pear, little lass!"

Thus blessings still dispenses the hand
Of Ribbeck at Ribbeck in Havelland.

*Helen Kurz Roberts*

*Conrad Ferdinand Meyer*

## NACH EINEM NIEDERLÄNDER

Der Meister malt ein kleines, zartes Bild,
Zurückgelehnt beschaut ers liebevoll.
Es pocht. „Herein." Ein flämischer Junker ists
Mit einer drallen, aufgedonnerten Dirn,
Der vor Gesundheit fast die Wange birst.
Sie rauscht von Seide, flimmert von Geschmeid.
„Wir habens eilig, lieber Meister. Wißt,
Ein wackrer Schelm stiehlt mir das Töchterlein.
Morgen ist Hochzeit. Malet mir mein Kind!"
„Zur Stunde, Herr! Nur noch den Pinselstrich!"
Sie treten lustig vor die Staffelei:
Auf einem blanken Kissen schlummernd liegt
Ein feiner Mädchenkopf. Der Meister setzt
Des Blumenkranzes tiefste Knospe noch
Auf die verblichne Stirn mit leichter Hand.
– „Nach der Natur?" – „Nach der Natur. Mein Kind.
Gestern beerdigt. Herr, ich bin zu Dienst."

## AFTER A DUTCH MASTER

The master paints a portrait, small but fine.
He stands aside and looks at it with love.
A knock. "Come in!" A Flemish baron leads
His daughter in: a coarse and gaudy wench
Whose rosy cheeks betoken perfect health.
Her silk gown rustles; her jewels flash light.
"Our time is precious, honored sir.
A lusty rogue intends to steal my girl from me.
Tomorrow they'll be wed. So paint my child!"
"At once, my Lord. Permit this final stroke."
With merry laugh they step before the easel.
Upon a cushion smooth, a lovely girl
Has laid her head. She sleeps. The master paints
With skillful hand the final flowret still,
Upon the leafy garland round the pale
And faded brow. "From life?" the baron asks.
"From life. My child. I buried her but
Yesterday . . . My lord, my time is yours."

*Daniel Coogan*

## DIE FÜSSE IM FEUER

Wild zuckt der Blitz. In fahlem Lichte steht ein Turm.
Der Donner rollt. Ein Reiter kämpft mit seinem Roß,
Springt ab und pocht ans Tor und lärmt. Sein Mantel saust
Im Wind. Er hält den scheuen Fuchs am Zügel fest.

Ein schmales Gitterfenster schimmert goldenhell,
Und knarrend öffnet jetzt das Tor ein Edelmann ...

„Ich bin ein Knecht des Königs, als Kurier geschickt
Nach Nîmes. Herbergt mich! Ihr kennt des Königs Rock!" –
„Es stürmt. Mein Gast bist du. Dein Kleid, was kümmerts mich?
Tritt ein und wärme dich! Ich sorge für dein Tier!"

Der Reiter tritt in einen dunkeln Ahnensaal,
Von eines weiten Herdes Feuer schwach erhellt,
Und je nach seines Flackerns launenhaftem Licht
Droht hier ein Hugenott im Harnisch, dort ein Weib,
Ein stolzes Edelweib aus braunem Ahnenbild ...

Der Reiter wirft sich in den Sessel vor dem Herd
Und starrt in den lebendgen Brand. Er brütet, gafft ...
Leis sträubt sich ihm das Haar. Er kennt den Herd, den Saal.
Die Flamme zischt. Zwei Füße zucken in der Glut.

Den Abendtisch bestellt die greise Schaffnerin
Mit Linnen blendend weiß. Das Edelmägdlein hilft.
Ein Knabe trug den Krug mit Wein. Der Kinder Blick
Hangt schreckensstarr am Gast und hangt am Herd entsetzt ...

Die Flamme zischt. Zwei Füße zucken in der Glut.
„Verdammt! Dasselbe Wappen! Dieser selbe Saal!
Drei Jahre sinds ... Auf einer Hugenottenjagd ...

THE FEET IN THE FIRE

A lightning flash. In its wan light a tower looms.
The thunder rolls. A horseman scarcely stays his mount,
Jumps off, raps on the gate and clamors. In the gale
Flutters his cloak. He grips his charger by the rein.

Out of a narrow wicket shines a golden light;
The creaking gate is opened by a nobleman.

"I am a servant of the King: a courier
Headed for Nêmes: you recognize his livery!"
"Foul weather! Be my guest. Your colors matter not.
Come in and warm yourself, while I see to your horse!"

The traveler enters in a dark ancestral hall;
An ample fireplace spreads a dim, uncertain light,
And as the fitful glimmer strikes the farther wall,
An armored Huguenot frowns here, a woman there,
A proud and noble lady, from the darkened frame. . . .

The traveler sinks into an armchair at the hearth
And looks into the vivid glow. He stares and broods. . . .
His hair is bristling now. He knows this hearth, this hall. . . .
A flame is hissing: two bare feet twitch in the blaze.

An aged housekeeper sets down the evening meal
On gleaming white damask. A noble maiden helps,
A boy brings in a jug of wine. The children gaze
In terror at the guest, in terror at the hearth. . . .

A flame is hissing: two bare feet twitch in the blaze.
"Damnation! The same hall, the self-same coat of arms!
It was three years ago . . . hunting for Huguenots . . .

Ein fein, halsstarrig Weib . . . ,Wo steckt der Junker? Sprich!'
Sie schweigt. ,Bekenn!' Sie schweigt. ,Gib ihn heraus!' Sie schweigt.
Ich werde wild. Der Stolz! Ich zerre das Geschöpf . . .
Die nackten Füße pack ich ihr und strecke sie
Tief mitten in die Glut . . . ,Gib ihn heraus!' . . . Sie schweigt . . .
Sie windet sich . . . Sahst du das Wappen nicht am Tor?
Wer hieß dich hier zu Gaste gehen, dummer Narr?
Hat er nur einen Tropfen Bluts, erwürgt er dich." –


Eintritt der Edelmann. „Du träumst! Zu Tische, Gast . . ."
Da sitzen sie. Die Drei in ihrer schwarzen Tracht
Und er. Doch keins der Kinder spricht das Tischgebet;
Ihn starren sie mit aufgerißnen Augen an.
Den Becher füllt und übergießt er, stürzt den Trunk,
Springt auf: „Herr, gebet jetzt mir meine Lagerstatt!
Müd bin ich wie ein Hund!" Ein Diener leuchtet ihm,
Doch auf der Schwelle wirft er einen Blick zurück
Und sieht den Knaben flüstern in des Vaters Ohr . . .
Dem Diener folgt er taumelnd in das Turmgemach.


Fest riegelt er die Tür. Er prüft Pistol und Schwert.
Gell pfeift der Sturm. Die Diele bebt. Die Decke stöhnt.
Die Treppe kracht . . . Dröhnt hier ein Tritt? Schleicht dort ein Schri
Ihn täuscht das Ohr. Vorüberwandelt Mitternacht.
Auf seinen Lidern lastet Blei, und schlummernd sinkt
Er auf das Lager. Draußen plätschert Regenflut.
Er träumt. „Gesteh!" Sie schweigt. „Gib ihn heraus!" Sie schweigt.
Er zerrt das Weib. Zwei Füße zucken in der Glut.
Aufsprüht und zischt ein Feuermeer, das ihn verschlingt . . .


„Erwach! Du solltest längst von hinnen sein! Es tagt!"
Durch die Tapetentür in das Gemach gelangt,
Vor seinem Lager steht des Schlosses Herr – ergraut,
Dem gestern dunkelbraun sich noch gekraust das Haar.

A brave and stubborn wife . . . 'Where is your man? Speak up!'
Silence. 'Confess!' Silence. 'Tell me!' Silence again.
It drives me wild. Such pride! I drag the creature down . . .
I grab her unshod feet and hold the two of them
Right in the fire . . . 'Where is your man?' Silence again . . .
She is convulsed . . . Didn't you see the crest outside?
Who told you to ask shelter here, you stupid fool!
If he has any guts in him he'll strangle you."

In comes the noble: "Dreaming? Come, to dinner, guest!"
And there they sit. The three of them in their black dress
And he. But neither of the children offers grace,
They just sit there and with their wide eyes stare at him –
He fills his cup to overflowing, spills the wine,
Jumps up: "My Lord, now show me to my resting place!
I am dog-tired!" A servant lights the way for him,
But on the door-sill he casts back a hurried glance
And sees the boy who whispers in his father's ear . . .
Then staggers he behind the servant to his room.

He bolts the door. He checks his pistol and his sword.
Shrill pipes the wind. The beams and boards quiver and groan.
The stairway creaks . . . Was that a step? . . . a stealthy tread?
His ears deceive him. Midnight comes at last and goes.
His lids are heavy now, he cannot stay awake
And falls abed. Outside, the splashing rain pours down.
He dreams. "Confess!" Silence. "Speak up!" Silence again.
He drags the woman. Two bare feet twitch in the fire.
Up flares the blaze, and he's devoured by hissing flames. . . .

"Wake up! You should long have been gone from here! It's day!"
A hidden door was opened in the tapestry
And there the manor's lord stood at his bed – gray-haired,
Although but yesterday his locks had been dark-brown.

Sie reiten durch den Wald. Kein Lüftchen regt sich heut.
Zersplittert liegen Ästetrümmer quer im Pfad.
Die frühsten Vöglein zwitschern, halb im Traume noch.
Friedselge Wolken schwimmen durch die klare Luft,
Als kehrten Engel heim von einer nächtgen Wacht.
Die dunkeln Schollen atmen kräftgen Erdgeruch.
Die Ebne öffnet sich. Im Felde geht ein Pflug.

Der Reiter lauert aus den Augenwinkeln: „Herr,
Ihr seid ein kluger Mann und voll Besonnenheit
Und wißt, daß ich dem größten König eigen bin.
Lebt wohl! Auf Nimmerwiedersehn!" Der andre spricht:
„Du sagsts! Dem größten König eigen! Heute ward
Sein Dienst mir schwer . . . Gemordet hast du teuflisch mir
Mein Weib! Und lebst! . . . Mein ist die Rache, redet Gott."

They're riding through the woods. Today the air is calm.
Broken and splintered boughs are strewn across their path.
The early birds are chirping, though yet half asleep,
And peaceful cloudlets drift along a clear blue sky
Like angels coming home from standing guard at night,
The moisture-darkened soil is fresh with earthy smell.

The traveler glances from the corner of his eye:
"My Lord, you are a truly wise and prudent man
And know me for a liegeman of the greatest king!
Farewell. You'll see me nevermore!" The other spoke:
"'Tis true! A liegeman of the Greatest King! Today
His service cost me much: you devilishly killed
My wife! and are alive! . . . Vengeance is Mine, says God."

*Martin Zwart*